How to
MEDITATE
with
CRYSTALS

About the Author

Jolie DeMarco is an international author, professional psychic, and metaphysical expert. She is a master of crystal healing and purposeful meditation. She's an inspirational speaker advocating wellness with a high-vibe lifestyle. She is president of My Flora Aura, a mindful meditation center and metaphysical retail space in Boca Raton, Florida. Jolie is the founder of www.Crystal Junkie.com, a retail website for learning and purchasing rocks and remedies. She is also a gifted medium and clairvoyant channel, giving more than one thousand readings per year. She has been featured on TLC for her psychic abilities and has authored over ten books, five oracle decks, phone applications, and several guided meditations to change your frequency. She can be viewed on Roku on *My Metaphysical Channel*. You can follow Jolie on Facebook, YouTube, and her podcasts.

How to MEDITATE *with* CRYSTALS

SIMPLE WAYS TO CHANGE YOUR LIFE

JOLIE DEMARCO

Llewellyn Publications
Woodbury, Minnesota

FIRST EDITION
First Printing, 2021

Cover design by Shannon McKuhen
Interior aura figure on page 25 and chakra figure on page 29 © Mary Ann Zapalac
Other interior illustrations by the Llewellyn Art Department

Llewellyn Publications is a registered trademark of Llewellyn Worldwide Ltd.

Library of Congress Cataloging-in-Publication Data
Names: DeMarco, Jolie, author.
Title: How to meditate with crystals : simple ways to change your life / Jolie DeMarco.
Description: First edition. | Woodbury, Minnesota : Llewellyn Publications, 2021. | Includes bibliographical references.
Identifiers: LCCN 2021008647 (print) | LCCN 2021008648 (ebook) | ISBN 9780738766744 (paperback) | ISBN 9780738766867 (ebook)
Subjects: LCSH: Meditation. | Crystals—Miscellanea.
Classification: LCC BL627 .D44 2021 (print) | LCC BL627 (ebook) | DDC 133/.2548—dc23
LC record available at https://lccn.loc.gov/2021008647
LC ebook record available at https://lccn.loc.gov/2021008648

Llewellyn Worldwide Ltd. does not participate in, endorse, or have any authority or responsibility concerning private business transactions between our authors and the public.

All mail addressed to the author is forwarded but the publisher cannot, unless specifically instructed by the author, give out an address or phone number.

Any internet references contained in this work are current at publication time, but the publisher cannot guarantee that a specific location will continue to be maintained. Please refer to the publisher's website for links to authors' websites and other sources.

Llewellyn Publications
A Division of Llewellyn Worldwide Ltd.
2143 Wooddale Drive
Woodbury, MN 55125-2989
www.llewellyn.com

Printed in the United States of America

Other Books by Jolie DeMarco

I dedicate this book to nature: the beautiful birds that sing every morning at my house, the lizards that make me look at their little cute bodies, my dogs that lie by me while I'm writing each day, the trees that clean our air, the running water, the environment of natural living, and a healthy life. I thank all of existence for allowing me to learn, teach, and share.

Contents

Part 2: Using Crystals during Meditation

Chapter 6: Best Crystals for Meditations   115

Part 3: Meditation Practices

Chapter 7: Meditations to Get Started   129

Chapter 8: Thirty-Three Meditations with Powerful Crystals 135

Disclaimer

The advice in this book is not meant to replace medical treatment. Please consult a medical professional for all physical and mental ailments and do not discontinue prescribed medications and/or treatments in favor of crystal healing.

Introduction

Most people don't realize how easy it is to meditate. Meditation has been a stress reliever and lifesaver to millions. The evidence seems clear: meditation lowers stress and helps your body heal. It also creates positive frequencies that can enhance your life. I say meditation is the best habit you can create.

Hi! I'm Jolie DeMarco, meditation master and crystal guru—at least, that is what people call me. I can teach you how to meditate easily. In this book, I offer you five effortless methods of meditation and provide thirty-three frequency-adjusting meditations that include simple directions and incorporate potent crystals that will take you to a euphoric level. These meditations can assist you in your life's needs. Let me show you the way to your bliss as I guide you to explore the worlds within your mind.

Before I begin, let me tell you that my definition of meditation is whenever you forget about time. Think of meditation as relaxing and reprograming with basically no effort. Time constricts and binds us to responsibilities. We all need structure in life, but we also need a break from conformity, like a mini vacation. Meditation is the mini vacation in your mind that protects you from those recurring thoughts. It brings you to a neutral state without worries or mental stressors, such as those thoughts of *What do I need to do today, next week, or by the end of the year?* I promise that meditating for ten to thirty minutes a day will propel your life into a blissful state of being. Hello, happy you!

Why Do We Meditate?

The point of meditation is to raise your frequency. We each have our own unique frequency that we give off. Other people may describe you as happy, sad, incredible, and so on. These are descriptive words, but they are sort of like a frequency you emit. Similarly, a song on the radio can make you happy, sad, or get you feeling sexy. All feelings are part of a frequency that is felt or noticed with your senses. Meditation is the perfect tool to change your frequency for the better. It releases stress and calms your body and mind. It strengthens your vitality and creates positivity in your life. Meditation also opens or renews passion, personal power, mind strength, advancement, and connection to one's inner self and higher source.

Frequencies are the rate at which something is repeated over a period of time. Imagine you are in a room with a bunch of people. One person shares a story about a negative situation they went through. Most people who listen to that sad story—that sad spoken frequency—are now thinking, imagining, or talking about their own negative occurrences. In turn, most people in that room are now on a lower frequency. If the speaker had shared a positive message, the vibration of the room would be at a higher frequency, which is a happier vibration. Frequencies can be matched or changed. The positive vibes we love to adapt to and keep, but some negative ones, such as abuse, bad thoughts of self, and bad behaviors, can also affect our frequency and bring us down. When a person has the will and self-realization to change, they change their frequency and create a new one.

Meditation can assist you in changing your frequency and advancing yourself, no matter if you have things to let go of, balance, or improve upon. All meditation is a mind retraining and release. If you just want to have peace and are not looking to change or tweak anything, meditation is also helpful for that purpose.

We all have different things going on in our lives, and I can attest that meditating helps me live happily. Here are my signs that I need, and I mean *need,* to meditate: when I hold my steering wheel too tightly, and when other people in my life dump their problems and I am the trash can. I also find when I am working on my computer for too long, I need to unplug. Are you feeling me out there? Another sign is when I just can't think or decide on anything. This means that I am unable to be in the present moment and that I am definitely not connected to the earth. I also need to meditate when I am feeling discouraged or need some self-power. I love to connect to my inner self or my archangels to pull me through the *woe is me* type of day. I especially meditate when I am overwhelmed or need to clear out my overthinking.

When you are sad, upset, and depressed, your vibrational energy is low. This is a perfect time to bring those vibes up and eliminate those negativities in mind—both your conscious and subconscious mind—by doing a releasing meditation, then choosing an uplifting or self-empowerment meditation afterward. Meditation can help you release any unwanted junk, renew your perceptions of life, calm anxiety and stress, help you with focus and structure, and, if you're interested, connect you with loved ones who have passed. Meditation gets you out of your funk quickly because you are the main ingredient. All you need to change is your own frequency. You can do this by creating new positive visions and thoughts. Hit the meditations to reach your bliss.

How Can Meditation Help Me Find Balance?

Meditation doesn't have to be a huge commitment; simply allowing yourself to do a relaxing task or go to a nothingness, mindless state of being can bring differences in your life. Exploring the five methods of meditation will help you discover what type of meditation suits your lifestyle. There are nonactive–slightly awake, active-awake, active physical body movement, mindful thoughts, and mindless meditations. You will connect with one or more to suit your purpose for that day. Any of these methods of meditation combined with crystals can create superior sessions, and the time you put in for yourself will surpass anything you imagined! Crystals bring adjusting energy frequencies to enhance your body's energy frequency; that is just one reason to utilize crystals with your meditation practices. We are all very different with our lifestyles, needs, and wants; this is why you can connect a certain purpose to each meditation and coordinating crystals to make the most of your newfound, powerful habit.

If you feel like something is missing in your life, meditation can help. But first you must address the void by recognizing what it is. There are three simple categories that can prove how balanced you are. For humans to be balanced, we must have these three categories as close to equal as we can, especially as we deal with time in our lives: self-passion, work, and relationships (romantic, familial, and friendly). In the next few pages, just for the fun of it, I will explain how to do a simple evaluation of your current frequency and guide you to see your level of contentment.

The first category is self-passion. Not sex passion, but self-passion. It is what you do for yourself, at least once a week, that you cannot wait to do! It can be as little as taking a walk or as big as painting a masterpiece. It just has to be for you, not something you do on the way to another task or for others. It is something that you solely do for yourself. We need self-passion to feel whole and keep our personal power. My self-passion is sitting under my tree in my backyard. I like to chill and look at the nature. My main self-passion is growing my crystal collection. I visit crystal shops and geological places where I instantly am surrounded by magical earth energies. This is something I look forward to doing monthly and sometimes weekly!

The second category is work—your job, your career, homemaking, and so on. You are still "putting time in" when you think or talk about work, even though you might not physically be there! Loving your work is the best way to know it is good for you. If you despise it, you may want to look into a job change. For some people, working out your body with exercise can be considered work! Others feel exercise belongs in the self-passion category.

The third category is relationships. This has subcategories: romantic partners, family, friends, and acquaintances. Visiting them, going places with them, and also talking on Zoom or the phone with them—this all counts as time spent with these people you have relationships with.

To find out if you are balanced, we are going to list the categories, and then you can see what you allow weekly for each. The total of the three categories will tell you where to spend more time to balance yourself. Each category should be the same amount of time.

On paper, write out the three categories. The first category is *self-passion*, the second is *work*, and the third is *relationships*. Once you have written down the three categories, list how much time you think you spend per week doing actions related to each category. Be honest. This will help you see if you are balanced or need some adjustments.

Looking at the weekly totals is the easiest way to see what areas of your life you can add to, release, or give more attention to. Doing this weekly can improve the balance of your time and true happiness.

Now, remember, some people may be passionate about working out, but others do it for their looks or health. If you are in the second group, you need to add that time under the work category because you are working for a goal of your body and health, not necessarily out of passion. On the other hand, if you are training for a self-passion purpose, like a 5k run that you love and enjoy, place this in the self-passion category. Calculate the time per week you spend doing or thinking of work.

The category of relationships will calculate the weekly time you spend with each of the subgroups. If there is no romantic relationship, such as a significant other, then that would be zero time.

Try to guesstimate to the best of your knowledge to get the gist of how balanced you are. Here is a big hint: if you are not happy or close to your contentment, most likely you are not balanced!

Remember, when calculating the time, just be honest. Don't make yourself crazy with the math. Look at the approximate hours, then notice which category or subcategory needs a bit more attention.

Check out the Unbalanced Time chart (page 6). It clearly shows this person lacks in self-passion and relationships in their current life. They work an inordinate amount of time, which means they are not making enough time to meet a person for love. It is very hard for someone to meet a good match if they have no self-passion and don't take actions to meet others. If this person would make efforts to grow self-passion two or three times a week, finding a self-passion such as walking on the beach or getting a coffee at a new place each week, they could become more balanced. It really is not hard to do; just realizing what you are currently doing or not doing opens your eyes to change. This first chart is an unbalanced person; the second chart is a well-balanced, healthy person. Remember, you don't have to fill every hour with the categories; look at how you feel, and when you change just slightly, you can notice a big difference in your happiness.

Unbalanced Time

Self-Passion	Work	Relationships
0 hours	70 hours	romantic 0 hours, family 12 hours, friends 3 hours

Balanced time

Self-Passion	Work	Relationships
11 hours	40 hours	romantic, family, and friends— all combined, at least 22 hours or more!

What's Contentment?

If you are feeling unbalanced, it will affect your contentment. Contentment brings you comfort and solace in your life. When I started meditating, I began to change for the better: my thoughts became more organized, I felt a connection to my sources, and I felt more loved than I had ever felt before in my life. This helped me be more successful in my work, relationships, and self-passion. It is your journey to find your contentment level and reach your potential. I will show you my meditation and crystal toolbox to get you there.

Anything that awakens your six senses to become happier and more positive in your thoughts and feelings can raise your frequency of contentment. This is your personal vibration of your mind, body, and soul.

Here are some easy ways to raise your vibration that take just a few seconds.

- Watch a beautiful sunset.
- Listen to a song that makes you feel happy.
- Visualize your own success.

- Think about something you love unconditionally, such as a pet, or holding your beloved pet for a few minutes.
- Sniff a flower that reminds you of a good, happy occasion. (Smelling an essential oil also places you in a great or relaxing mood. Pick something that triggers a positive mindset.)
- Drink something that is refreshing.

There is one extraordinary being whom I consider one of my sources from the angelic realm; his name is Archangel Michael. I had never heard of him until I was in my late thirties and on my spiritual path. He is said to be closest to God, or your source. He is known as a protector and possesses all-knowing information for the greater good of all life. I adapted clairvoyant abilities and hear from him through my spiritual meditations. He teaches me life lessons and shares insights to guide and assist me on Earth and to be my best self. In my awake meditations, he shares lots of knowledge about human relationships, particularly relationships with oneself. Archangel Michael talks of levels of contentment. We as humans have different levels of what makes us happy, especially as we all come from different locations of the world, different families, and different traditions and life experiences that created who we are today as well as our current frequency. Learned behaviors are harder to change, but nonetheless, we are all retrainable if we allow ourselves and give ourselves permission to be retrained. Keeping your willpower and soul connection will result in easy transformations. After all, it's just a frequency!

There is another way you can gauge your frequency other than the contentment chart, but before we get there, let's figure out a purpose that can connect you with the perfect meditation practice.

How Do You Meditate with Purpose?

You have reached inside and found out that meditation can be practiced many ways using crystals, the importance of balancing, and your level of contentment. Now, it's appropriate to find the right type of meditation to practice. This will be easiest when you identify what your purpose or intention for practicing meditation is. Doing a meditation with purpose can enhance your lifestyle. For example, it can help you reach personal and work goals. Meditating can be done for many purposes, and there is a meditation to adjust your frequency for every situation. For example, you might meditate to release energy, to reconnect with your whole self, to calm stress and anxiety, to help you focus, or to connect with loved ones who have passed on. These are some of the topics and purposes for meditations that appear in this book.

Releasing Meditations

There are many ways to release energy that keeps us stuck and junked up, so to speak. I have created more than one way to release energy that no longer serves you. Once you have identified your specific purpose, you can match what type of release you will do. An emotional release is quite different from a physical one. Learning to meditate is simple if you allow it and give yourself permission to do it.

I teach that release and let-go meditations should be followed by a gratitude meditation. This is to fill in the voids of where and what you released with positive vibrations. Whatever energy you let go of needs to be replaced with something positive, otherwise you will feel off or empty. It is best to immediately fill that energetic space. This way, you don't let that old energy you released come back!

Renew Your Perceptions of Life

The connection to your higher self is a gift. The gift is that we all have access to all of our existence. This explains why once in a while you may feel unbalanced or disconnected from yourself or your life. This disconnection is most likely because you have a void in at least one department of your life. It happens to all of us at one time or another; it's normal to be unbalanced from time to time. If we were not unbalanced once in a while, we would not know how to appreciate life or feel that need to be happier.

Archangel Michael taught me through visualization and autowriting messages how we humans can erase negative vibrational patterns that we learned from our environment, which includes our family, friends, work, and all our experiences. He explained that we come into this world clean and clear, but we've adopted and accepted certain behaviors and actions to become who we are in the present day. We pick up other people's emotions and own them; we learn things we thought were facts and decide if we want to allow them to influence our lives.

All in all, Archangel Michael expressed that we all have the power to change frequencies. We can decide to clean, clear, and balance them in our lifetime. Sometimes there is no immediate poof you are healed, but the power of thoughts and actions can get you to a "normal" place—at least, your normal, and what you want to accept as your normal at this point in your life.

Calm Anxiety and Stress

We all can use remedies, especially to calm ourselves from everyday stressors. For some, it is hard to pinpoint what makes them stressed, since most people work daily and feel pressure but don't identify that as stress. Let's just look at what you do on a daily basis—just for giggles.

Write down every task you do for one day. Here, we'll go along with the example of one woman who initially thought she wasn't stressed at all.

You wake up, make your children's beds, make them breakfast and lunch for school, drop two kids off at one school and the other two about ten miles away at another school. You rush to work—another thirty minutes of driving. You have a customer service job where you are fielding problems all day. At 3:00 p.m., you rush to pick up your children from both schools, help them with homework, make dinner, clean up, make sure they are ready for bed, and work a second online job from 7:00 to 10:00 p.m.

I'm getting stressed just writing this out on paper! We didn't even get to the laundry and other daily household tasks and her significant other yet! Holy heavens—I think her issues are from overdoing it.

Once you identify that you are having an anxious or a stressful day, you can better recognize the purpose of using meditation to reset your frequency.

In each meditation in this book, you will notice that it starts with breathing in and out. When more oxygen is in our system, it calms our bodies and can slow the feeling of being rushed or anxious, because its rhythm helps our body functions flow in a healthy cycle. Breath work can be a simple technique to regulate your system and relax you. In chapter 8, try the Meditation for Focus, Mental Stability, and Calm.

Help with Focus and Structure

Have you ever felt like everything is out of your control and you are losing all sense of your being? This feeling can come from an identity crisis or just a simple change of job or relationship. All changes can potentially result in the loss of focus and structure. Focus and structure are easy to gain back or create, though. If you never had much focus or structure, using meditations for purpose will help you notice with ease.

These meditations can be relaxing and mindful. Getting your thoughts in some type of order can get you set for success. Resetting your frequencies to be stationary, at least for a few moments, keeps you grounded. "Grounded space" means that you are at least slightly aware or fully aware in that present moment. I diligently work on my focus because I am an empath. An empath is super sensitive to emotions and environments, connecting to them with all their senses. I make sure I give myself at least fifteen minutes or more a day to notice my feet touching the ground and to mindfully say, "I am happy to be present on Earth." This little exercise brings structure and focus in my day.

If you would like to add extra power to focus and align yourself to your daily tasks or goals, hold a white howlite stone. This stone is a strong provider of structure and positive conformity. It absorbs many emotions that get us offtrack, such as anger and insomnia. Howlite calms you and can help you with studying or general focus. If you struggle with ADD or ADHD, white howlite is a main crystal to use in the process of self-healing and calming unruly energy. If you only need a bit of grounding, I would suggest a hematite stone. This has the element of earth, helps memory, and stimulates original thoughts while limiting overthinking. It also helps with breaking free from self-sabotage and self-limitations. A focus meditation with crystals is powerful and creates organized thoughts and practices. Your intent is evident and clear after a meditative session.

Connect with Loved Ones Who Have Passed

Most of us have experienced the loss of a person with whom we were physically or emotionally connected, and we miss their touch, smell, and comradery. It can be hard. But we can remain connected to family members and friends who have passed over into the light by energetically connecting to their vibrations and frequencies. To do this, we must first get ourselves on a high vibration, a frequency that can be heard and will link us together once again, like a phone call or a "presence visit." You can raise your vibrations many ways (explained in chapter 3). You can also add your crystals!

Spirit quartz is a combination of amethyst and citrine and looks like a cactus. This crystal elevates your energy, all your chakras, and all layers of your aura to make attaining frequencies for communication and/or visitation easier. Enhance the vibes further by adding unakite—a green-and-pink-speckled stone—to the meditation. This incredible stone brings the heart and mind to love and kindness frequencies, which are extremely high frequencies. Unakite balances your emotions and creates healing within the emotional energy layer of your aura to help you connect to your deceased loved one as you are feeling many emotions for them.

Usually during these meditations, my mind takes me to see and have a conversation with my loved one. I allow it and accept the words or feelings and visions to come; I don't overthink, and I am peaceful. I may receive just one word or thought. But I know it was from them touching my energy with love. I have also felt like I have been brushed with a hand or touched on my head, as if they were letting me know they have arrived and connected with me. Some visitations can last for twenty minutes, while others can last less than five minutes. I am grateful for whatever is available. I conclude my meditation with those who have passed over by telling them I love them and will see them next time! It is a gift that we all can revisit those we have lost on the earthly plane and find peace by knowing their vitality is infinite.

As you explore incredible meditations with purpose and true intent, you may find that you become more content, creative, successful, and inventive. Let's begin learning about meditation to assist you in your physical healing and create overall wellness.

Why It's Helpful to Incorporate Crystals into Your Meditations

It seems we all love to supersize everything. Commercially, you can get everything bigger, with extra power and gusto. In the metaphysical world, it's more about what tool works best for your energy. That leads me to crystals, the favorite tool of any metaphysician. Crystals are amazing earth compositions that hold and emit frequencies, just as humans can hold and emit frequencies. Humans and crystals work well together! Crystals can help release, adjust, and balance a human's frequency with its own energies.

People can use meditation practices to change their frequency and crystals to supersize the outcome and make a wonderful experience. Just as there are certain practice options of meditation, there are also certain crystals that match up to your purpose to create the ultimate experience. I joke around, saying crystals are natural vitamins for the body and soul. I really do mean that they help you become healthier. Having worked with clients for over eleven years in crystal meditation and healing sessions, I have found that crystals help people who use them for physical, emotional, mental, and spiritual balancing, healing, and advancement.

Crystal healing involves the placement of crystals near or on the human body. This is a true holistic modality. It is no new discovery. Crystals have been used for healing and protection since the beginning of time. Using crystal energy is amazing, especially when you are the person discovering the powers crystals can emit! That is a grand occurrence in itself. A crystal experience never gets old for me. I am in awe of how crystals changed my life and the lives of many others. In this book, the combinations of crystals have been carefully chosen to optimize your purpose and method of meditation.

As you explore incredible meditations with purpose and true intent, you may find that you become more content, creative, successful, and inventive. In part 1, we'll get into the basics and methods of meditation, as well as tools that can boost your meditation practice. In part 2, we'll go deeper into why crystals are such a supportive tool for your meditation practice. From there, you'll discover thirty-three powerful crystals to use with meditation, as well as thirty-three guided crystal meditations. Let's begin learning about meditation with crystals to assist you in physical healing and creating overall wellness!

Part 1

Meditation Made Easy

Chapter 1
The Basics of Meditation

I bet you've heard about meditation programs. Most instructors tell you to relax and suggest that you empty your mind. If that is how they are telling you to meditate, it doesn't seem very helpful.

Meditation is not just leaving all things out of your mind; it is truly a way of life—well, in a sense. Let me explain. Meditation is basically when you just *forget about time* and allow yourself to go to a blissful state. Another descriptive word is *autopilot*, or performing an action that you naturally do without thinking about what your body is doing. The basics start with not only teaching you to empty your mind, but also sharing the benefits of and answering all your questions about meditation: how energy and frequencies work, the importance of comfort and the length of meditations, and specifics of your chakras and aura layers. I added a sweet challenge for you to have fun with your frequency and topped it with some stunning types of meditation. Monocycle, guided, and manifesting meditations will rock your world.

The Benefits of Meditation

Did we want to get into some research regarding why meditation is great for your health? Yes? Okay, let's go there.

Meditation twice a week lowers stress and may increase your life span. Those are pretty incredible outcomes from allowing yourself to have a mini vacation. Johns Hopkins University in Baltimore, Maryland, did nineteen thousand studies on meditation and found that mindful meditation can help physiological stressors like anxieties, depression, and pain.[1] Dr. Elizabeth Hoge, a physiatrist and assistant professor at Harvard, says that mindful meditation makes perfect sense for treating anxiety: "People with anxiety have a problem dealing with distracting thoughts that have too much power ... They can't distinguish between a problem-solving thought and a nagging worry that has no benefit."[2] She points out that if you have these kinds of worries, it's possible to change your experience with training. As you read this book, you will get the information you need to retrain those unruly thoughts and get yourself back in your own thought power, or what most of us call "mindfulness."

There are additional benefits to meditating. Meditation can be used for certain purposes, and, of course, each one will set a vibrational frequency for you to connect and adapt to. Meditation can elevate your vibration; for example, a self-advancing meditation can be used for manifesting, betterment, or projection of goals. How about releasing old energy? Meditation can help you use your senses to let go.

Basic meditations can uplift you as well as help you release tension and stress—all these benefits are surely needed. Meditation can additionally motivate you, adjust your mindset to be more positive, help you manifest, take you on enlightening mind journeys, and give you insight or epiphanies.

I believe that we can change our path in life. We can do this by manifesting our desires and wants with unwavering beliefs and positive connections to those desires. Truly feeling in our heart that we deserve what we desire will bring those desires to fruition.

Meditation also connects you to guides, angels, Mother Earth, Father Sky, and your god or source. The techniques I will show you can help you speak stronger to your soul and become fantastic at all your tasks, careers, and rela-

1. Julie Corliss, "Mindfulness Meditation May Ease Anxiety, Mental Stress," *Harvard Health Publishing,* January 8, 2014, https://www.health.harvard.edu /blog/mindfulness-meditation-may-ease-anxiety-mental-stress-201401086967.

2. Ibid.

tionships. Above all, meditation raises your vibrational frequencies! Your frequency is your level of happiness. The ultimate goal is to appreciate the happiness in your life.

Emptying Your Mind

If you have tried to empty your mind but weren't given an explanation how to do it, I can clear that up for you. First of all, what does "clear your mind" really mean? It sounds simple, right? But it is kind of difficult if you try too hard.

Trying is the best way *not* to meditate. I say this because you will be thinking of how to do it. Thinking of how to meditate is distracting, and meditation is mindless. By that, I mean meditation is not thinking, not worrying, and not consciously experiencing.

Emptying your mind is when you are doing actions without thought or when you are not thinking about time. It's like listening to a person speak but not really hearing them. I think you know what I mean. Tune out. We have all tuned someone out at some point in our lives.

Most of you have probably tuned out during a task as well. Let me use the example of driving a car. At first when learning how to drive, it took a bit of time to get used to. You learned all the rules of the road, how to use the gas pedal and the brake and the turn signals, how to read signage, and so on. But then three or so years later, you drive mindlessly, kind of like you are on autopilot. You just perform the motions without thinking. You are driving, and the next thing you know, you are at your destination. I'm not suggesting you try meditation while driving. But it happens, and I'm using this example because I feel we all can relate.

Let me put it another way: simple tasks that you fully immerse yourself in can be a kind of meditation. Have you ever cooked or baked mindlessly and found that there was a great meal on the plate in front of you? You forgot about time and just did the task without thinking. Yeah, I know it's really *that* simple.

A daydream is that time lapse where you go somewhere in your mind as you are sitting. You may not remember anything afterward; it is a moment when you go mindless or to what I call "mind space." That daydream of nothingness is a form of mindless meditation. If you do, however, remember the daydream, that would be a slightly-awake meditation.

Years ago, I was in the flower business. I owned a flower shop and designed beautiful arrangements of roses, orchids, hydrangeas, and daises. You name it, and I designed them into beautiful creations of art. I would start by gathering all the items I needed. The next thing I knew, my mother, who helped me often, would walk into the flower shop and say, "Jolie, it's eight at night! You have been designing flowers for six hours. Don't you know what time it is?" I was lost in my beautiful creations; I couldn't tell you where my mind went. But I don't remember holding the clippers or making the twenty arrangements that were in front of me. I *loved* to design flowers. It made me happy, and nothing else mattered around me. I guess you can say it was a passion of mine.

As these examples illustrate, meditation doesn't have to be a huge commitment. It is small amounts of you simply allowing yourself to *do*. A relaxing task or a mindless state of being can bring BIG differences in your life. Meditation is the best habit you can create.

Frequently Asked Questions about Meditation

I noticed that when I teach meditation classes to beginners, they have lots of questions. Some of the questions seem simplistic; however, not everyone is on the same level or frequency. In fact, some students have no idea what frequency or energy is. Many don't understand how it can positively affect us. Once you know, life gets easier.

What Is Energy and Frequency

Let's start with energy. This is a statement I use that says it all: "Everything that exists has energy." Also, "Energy, in physics, the capacity for doing work. It may exist in potential, kinetic, thermal, electrical, chemical, nuclear, or other various forms. There are, moreover, heat and work—i.e., energy in the process of transfer from one body to another."[3] All people consist of, absorb, and emit vibrational energy, just like a rock, a crystal, or anything on Earth. I can attest to the existence of energy beyond Earth as well (more on that later).

---

3. "Energy," *Britannica*, https://www.britannica.com/science/energy.

Back to energy and frequency. If everything is energy, then it makes sense that everything will have a frequency. Let's say your body's energy can be transferred and measured by your actions, thoughts, and surroundings. That means your frequency can actually change from second to second. For example, if you enter a blue room, you may get a feeling of *ahhh*—a relaxing vibe. That may change your frequency from what is was before you entered the blue room. Energy can come from objects in our environment; the same goes for people in our life. There is more: what we verbally say is a vibration, and so are our thoughts. They are frequencies that emit from you. They can be directed at the self or at other people or things. If I said a negative word to you, it may make you mad, upset, or possibly want to say a negative or nice word back. These interactions cause change in the frequency of our body's energy. All these examples are energy exchanges. This is teaching you that everything truly is energy. It attests to how we can strive to make positive choices in our words, tones, attitudes, and actions because they affect us and other people in our lives. Meditation not only can help us keep a balance of our body and mind, but also of our actions and reactions in everyday life. Crystals and purposeful meditations become useful as both can derail any offsets and bring you to incredible changes.

Now, think of frequency like a value. Your vibrational energy is low when you are sad, upset, and depressed. Frequencies can be pretty much matched, or they can be changed when energy is exchanged to shift your body, mind, and soul. Experiences affect us. For example, one hour of self-care can give equal happiness, which is the abundance of the self-passion aspect of your life. This can be quite significant, as you noticeably feel that you are more balanced mentally and emotionally for giving yourself one hour of time. A vibrational frequency that ignites your soul or your imagination can reveal new perspectives.

How Do I Sync My Body and Mind?

To really connect, we must first sync up the body and mind. In other words, the conscious and the subconscious. The *conscious* part of you is the "human" you—the skin and bones, the physical part of you that is standing on Earth right now. The you that makes mental and emotional decisions and takes action (standing still, taking, gifting, accepting, forgiving, circling in patterns, etc.). We strive to always move in positive and admirable directions in our life. This is why it is important to meditate and connect "all of you"—to be on the same frequency as your desires and goals. This keeps you balanced and happy.

Your *subconscious* is the soul connection of your energy. It is the vibrational part of you that will always exist. Your subconscious energy is an all-knowing part of you. The higher self is the positive part of the subconscious. This is the unconditional loving part that only sends you helpful information, visions, and perspectives. The idea here is that you can receive feelings, visions, or knowledge that can help you lead a happier, easier life. The subconscious is guiding you to make better choices and balance your behaviors to be kinder, lighter, and more positive in your life flow.

When you connect, you are ultimately your own best friend. This best friend knows everything about you. The higher self of you only wants the best for you and will never drive you to or suggest anything other than positive ways of looking at a situation. Your higher self is helping you have the perspective to solve problems and be the best you can possibly be.

Do I Have to Sit in a Yoga Pose?

Along with the energy and frequency questions, I am also asked if everyone needs to sit in that yoga position to meditate. Sitting in a cross-legged position is fine, but it is not the only way to meditate. All you have to do is find your "comfort zone," which is any place in which you feel relaxed. This may be sitting in a chair, lying on a bed, or leaning back in a recliner; it is up to you. The position of your body is not really a factor, other than your personal comfort.

The comfort zone applies to more than just your sitting position. It also includes your environment, which can affect your meditations. Our five senses play a huge part in allowing meditation to get us to that mind space we need.

Meditation can be affected by noise and sound. Some sounds that can enhance meditation include water, ambiance music, sound bowls, or birdsong. Influencing smells can include lavender, cookies, and so on. Taste can affect meditation. This may sound silly, but if I have gum in my mouth, it puts me in my comfort space; in contrast, if I eat a sub with onions an hour before my meditation, the onion taste in my mouth overtakes my comfort zone and I can't get to my mind space. Touch—such as the textures of the furniture I am sitting on or the feeling of a velvet jacket—and sight—a rainbow, a blue room, a beautiful beach, and so on—can also be factors that enhance or distract from your meditation.

You should experiment to see what atmosphere gets you to that comfortable mind space. Being relaxed and thinking positive keep you on high vibrations of happiness. Meditation brings the high vibrational frequencies that calm and relax, then allow connection and happy space.

How Long Do I Have to Meditate?

Some have asked me how long a meditation has to be to benefit from it. My answer: one minute. Seriously. Some people can benefit from one minute because they can set their thoughts in a nice package or Zen space within that amount of time. But that comes with practice and knowledge. Realistically, there is no right or wrong answer. I think a really great meditation lasts between twenty and sixty minutes. In this book, we are working with crystals as boosters for meditation; this means your session will have extra power adaptors to help you.

Generally, meditation is best when performed for at least twenty minutes. Think about this: it usually takes a person at least ten minutes to unwind from daily activities, so twenty minutes really isn't very long. Gift the time to yourself and think of it like an unconditional appointment of love and advice—like a consultation from an expert!

In this book, I provide thirty-three different meditations, and all vary in length. If you have limited time, aim for twenty minutes the first few times. You may feel ten minutes is good, too. The better you get, the longer your sessions may become, as you may want to travel out-of-body or receive more information from guides or angels! If you love it, you will find yourself drawn to connection more often.

What Are Auras?

Let's talk a little more about energy. We all have our physical body and our energetic body. Your physical body is made up of your cells, blood, bones, and so on. Then, you have this unseen layer of energy vibration that extends two to three feet out and around your physical body. Yep. You are bigger than you thought, huh? This electromagnetic field (EMF) around the human body is considered the energetic body, also known as the aura.

Our aura has layers to it, which are the energetic vibrational fields. Each layer can absorb, hold, or emit any other vibrations that connect with it. I break the aura down into four layers.

- The first layer, closest to your skin and physical body, is the physical or etheric energy layer. This is where you actually feel with touch.
- The second layer is the emotional energy body that can hold or emit your feelings. Emotions are frequencies that can be suspended in one's auric field.
- The third layer is the mental energy body, which is where the process of *how* you think about things takes place.
- The fourth auric layer is the spiritual energy body, which is your connection to your past on this earthly plane or on any other planes (if you believe in past lives or parallel existence). Blockages or gifts are held in this energetic field as a frequency. An example would be a childhood trauma or an occurrence that you can't identify in this lifetime (meaning it was a frequency embedded from a past or parallel lifetime).

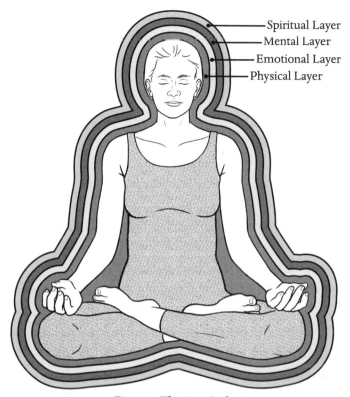

Spiritual Layer
Mental Layer
Emotional Layer
Physical Layer

Figure 1: The Aura Body

The aura is connected to our physical body but unseen to most human eyes. Some talented humans can see auras. (I can! I can!) Actually, we all can see and feel them! It just takes practice.

Just for fun, notice how much you feel from other people without asking them what is going on in their lives. Just stand next to a person and notice if you feel anything from their aura. Please don't make anyone feel uncomfortable by doing this. Remember your manners and respect others!

Okay, back to you! You can hold positive or negative frequencies in your energy field. The science of this is quite amazing. Think of your heartbeat and your blood flow; they have their own unique frequency to keep everything working well inside you. All the organs work with the inner body, and those same frequencies work with your outer body as well. All of you affects all of you. There are things that you may not necessarily be able to see visually with the human eye, but they can affect you inside and outside.

My life's experiences created frequencies, and I knew that I wanted to switch out a few of them. I used the lessons of those frequencies, adapted, and scooted out those negative frequencies. I rid myself of junk and only kept the positive frequencies. This raised my frequency by two notches. This way, I reached my bliss point, which is my magical level of current contentment.

We can get off-kilter if we have something traumatic occur or have emotional upsets. These are just things that happen in our lives. Knowing about your aura layers leads you to know where you may be holding unwanted frequencies that can disrupt your balance. Balancing all layers that surround your body is key to your happiness. Adjusting your own energy is a common courtesy to others. We don't want to pass on negative or low vibrations. Strive for positivity and harmony. Keep yourself on high vibrations through meditation.

Earlier in my life, I decided to get on that bandwagon and change. I meditated and figured out that, hey, this works for me. I actually found myself loving meditation. As I've aged, I've realized I will always have to do my maintenance, which is meditation. Meditation raised my frequency to another level of contentment. It gets me to the highest, happiest frequency that this earth will allow me.

The knowledge I have about different types of meditation methods comes from experimentation over the years. There are five main methods that bring you to meditate easily. While practicing the methods of meditation, I noticed that working with some of Mother Earth's frequencies helped adjust me. I am talking about crystals (or earth chunks, as I call them).

These modalities can assist in cleaning your auric field. Doing a self-meditation or voice-guided meditation is beneficial to balance and heal your energy system. You can balance your mind, physical body, and energetic body (the aura) easily within twenty minutes. When doing a self-meditation, performing a guided meditation, or receiving Reiki, you can also positively realign and balance your chakras.

Ready for a Challenge?

Once you understand how energy and thoughts affect you, it is time for you to identify your current frequency. Every day we wake up, we can create our own new frequency. Yes, it is true—we are sort of embedded with a frequency from our lifestyles, environment, and upbringing, but we can choose to adjust it. After all, we are the keeper of our mind, body, and soul, which are energy vibrations that create our own unique frequency. I really don't like calling this a "challenge" because that sounds like work, and meditation is not work, it's a self-gift. It is actually incredibly easy; it's like drinking a glass of water, because it is so replenishing and refreshing. Here we go.

Let's figure out what your frequency is right now. Before a meditation, it's cool to track your energy level and frequency. When you write these down in your journal, it shows how you progressed from day to day. Here is the simple way to track your current frequency: on a scale of one to ten, one being the lowest vibe and ten being a fabulous mood and amazingly positive mindset.

If you wake up and say, *Today my frequency is a seven!* write it down in your journal. Then, choose a meditation that fits your need for that day. After your meditation, notice if your frequency has changed. Most likely, it will be at least one level higher than when you started. That is a success! It can be a big jump or a slight jump in how your frequency changes. This proves that *you* are the master of you! Once you reach the number ten for more than seven days in a row, you are considered a meditation master!

Chakras and Color Meditation

While learning about meditations or practices such as yoga, you will hear people talk of chakras. These wheel- or disklike energy centers are located down the center of a person's body along the meridian or spinal column. Each chakra point is also associated with a color.

There are seven main chakras, but there are more than 144,000 chakras in the human body. Each chakra represents a center point in the human body that can energize, release, hold, or vibrate. These energy centers constantly open and close. Chakras can also change every time you have a positive or negative thought. This is normal, as our egos are basically a frequency of how we feel about *self*—the higher the frequency, the stronger our self-opinion, and vice versa.

Keeping chakras balanced is the key to being a balanced human. When I say balanced, I mean physically, mentally, emotionally, and spiritually. It is easy to balance; we can do it with our thoughts. Then those thoughts adjust our feelings and perceptions.

If a chakra is out of place for a long period of time, sickness can manifest. This sickness could be physical, mental, emotional, or spiritual. Keeping *yourself* and your chakras aligned and balanced is a must.

Let's look at the chakras and what they represent.

- The chakra at the base of the spine is called the root or first chakra. This chakra represents *grounding*, being in the now, the present moment, and wanting to be on Earth. It is represented by the color red. I sometimes visualize it as a deep, dark red.

- The second chakra is named the sacral chakra. It represents survival, instinct, and creativity, along with our sexual organs. It is seen as an orange color.

- The third chakra is the solar plexus. It represents personal power, emotions, and your ego. This chakra is yellow.

- The fourth chakra is the heart chakra. This area represents love and compassion for self and for others. The heart chakra is green or light pink.

- The fifth chakra is the throat chakra, representing communication, expression, and creativeness. It also represents being heard by other people, being expressive, and speaking your truth. It is represented as light blue.

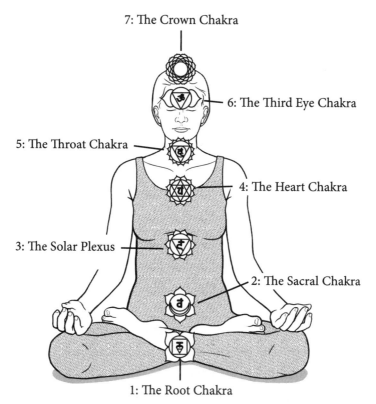

7: The Crown Chakra

6: The Third Eye Chakra

5: The Throat Chakra

4: The Heart Chakra

3: The Solar Plexus

2: The Sacral Chakra

1: The Root Chakra

Figure 2: The Seven Chakras

- The sixth chakra represents the third eye or mind's eye. This is your intuition and self-trust. This chakra is a deep indigo. The third eye is also called your sixth sense because, when awakened, it activates awareness. The third eye is located between the eyebrows. It can physically feel as if you have pressure on that area; some people feel like something is creating an almost hurt feeling there. This feeling is also described as if someone placed a sticker there! Personally, when my third eye is activated, I feel achy, like a tunnel or vortex is open there. But honestly, it feels kind of cool, because my brain is being harnessed.

- Last is the seventh chakra, called the crown. It represents connection to your higher self and is located at the crown of your head. Some feel the connection to energies of light and your source, whom your belief system recognizes as a higher power. Some believe in the *higher self,* which is the all-knowing part of you. You can also connect with the celestial plane of angels, spirit guides, and humans who have passed over or are on other dimensions. The crown chakra is white or gold but is often visualized or felt as violet.

The more you know about your body, the more it can help you stay balanced on the physical, emotional, and mental levels. If you are "seeing" or feeling colors in your mind's eye, that can be relaxing and informational. You may be connecting with a chakra color—that's very telling about what may be going on with you physically, emotionally, mentally, or spiritually.

Focusing on colors or your own body keeps you focused on one thing, not five trillion other things. Whenever you start thinking of your grocery lists or chores during meditation, bring your focus back to a body part or color.

Start by imagining both. First, focus on the center of your chest. This is easy for everyone to visualize. This is also the area of the heart chakra. Now, visualize and imagine the color green at the same time. Imagine feeling your body without touching it physically. Just notice that area by focusing your thought at the center of your chest. Then, imagine a green light in that spot, and start to feel or visualize your happy place or passion for something you love. Good. You got it. When you imagine the green light and your chest, you are keeping your focus on you. This keeps the mind chatter out. No hamster wheels are allowed here. If you practice that technique, you will *not* have to think about it. You know, like driving that car mindlessly. The actions just happen.

Another way to use color to balance you within five minutes is this rainbow self-healing technique. Imagine a rainbow of beautiful colors, all hues.

Then imagine all those amazing colors washing over your entire body from the top of your head to the bottoms of your feet. Then say, "Anything other than the light will go out of my body and energy field into the earth to be recycled and renewed." You did it! You are clean and clear. By the way, in my world, if you can visualize a colorful rainbow, you are going to be successful at anything you set your mind to!

Types of Meditation

Now that we have covered some basics, there are many techniques and purposes for meditation. Knowing why you want to meditate is your best bet as far as inviting yourself into an amazing alternate atmosphere, world, or enlightenment of self and your overall presence. These meditation techniques will knock your socks off and possibly get you into outer space. No pressure.

There are different meditations for different purposes. Certain meditations can elevate your vibration. There are meditations that release old energy, packaging past experiences and providing closure so that we can forget and move on. There are relaxing meditations, where thoughts bring the body and breath into bliss. There are also healing meditations, and they work on physical, emotional, mental, and spiritual levels.

One example of mental healing is reprogramming or focusing on the polarity balance of the body and its parts or changing your thought process about anything you are holding on to at that moment. Using your mind to change perspective is one cool way to do that. If I were thinking of a person who disturbed my day, I would immediately pretend I was looking through their eyes. I would create a backstory and make a better scenario so that we could both let go of that negative encounter. Then, I would switch our story into a fun, happy one.

Another mental meditation example would be if you are a person who is always feeling alone. I allow myself to connect to a spirit guide or source, such as an angel or a god, and connect to them energetically with a white string of light, allowing them to send me a message, a thought, or a picture. The order of your progression comes from what you allow yourself to accomplish.

Manifesting Meditations

I want to share some details about manifestation. The most common mani-festing purposes include money, wealth and abundance, a love relationship, and a job or life shift. I attest that manifesting meditations are incredibly effective if you follow the directions!

I feel at times that it is one of my tasks in this lifetime to teach all humans, as many as I can, how to manifest desires with equal energy exchange. As I wrote that last part, I felt like there was cool music playing, similar to the theme of *Star Wars* or *The Big Bang Theory*... must be in my head. Or the spirit guides are messing with me again. That is quite possible, as they have a great sense of humor!

I have come across many people who think manifesting is totally a one-way street. A me, me, me asking of the universe. Let me share why it is not. Let's say you are manifesting a love relationship. You try to manifest every-thing you want in that mate: the good looks, the kindness, the loyalty—you get what I mean. Then, you meet and get together—but your partner gets over you, because, although they fulfill all your desires, you may not fulfill theirs. I'm just saying, you have to connect with this point of giving as well as receiving.

Well, I am making it simple to manifest. I was specifically advised by the higher educated beings and angels. Basically, all those energies of the light (positive energy) that want us humans to succeed. They give us plenty of tools to be happier in our lives on Earth. Here is their advice for fruitful man-ifesting (just know that these guides joke a lot with me):

Humans create their own chaos. They have to realize what they want before asking and manifesting. We hear them continuously asking, but they are hardly specific and hardly feel they deserve it.

Maybe they weren't joking. I guess it's up to us humans to figure out what we want and need, then manifest it! Here is how to specifically man-ifest. You can follow the guidelines, and, of course, you can add what you like or take out some things according to your preference. You might want to grab a notebook and pen to figure out what you want, and then choose what your goals are to start.

Please remember the most important part. *Do not*, I repeat, *do not* take out the equal energy exchange! That was a message I just heard from the angels. Oh, by the way, these angels just told me that some of you reading this book are saying to yourself, "Who am I to ask such high spirits like angels or God to help me?"

They allow you to ask for what you want. It is not being selfish. Understand that all people deserve good things in life. That includes you! Make sure when you ask the angels for what it is you need that you are as specific as possible. They get a lot of requests and they want to bring what is needed.

There is importance in stating your true desire and intention and knowing you deserve what you are asking for. Everything we say—aloud or in our head—is energy. When doing your manifesting meditation, say what you want, but if afterward you think, "If it's meant to be, it will happen, or maybe it will come true," that is a big no-no! You instantly negated what you asked for by not believing it would happen and by placing uncertain energy that is negative or null. That means you just wasted your time! The manifesting message was distorted and won't get to the angels!

I have noticed that many of my clients fear being alone or not being able to make enough money, and so on. Fear places negative vibrations on your manifesting, and you know what that means! It means the energy you are sending out is uncertain and it is a lower frequency. This will not bring you what you need, want, or desire. Lose the fear! Be confident and know it will happen if you put the effort in the energy you send out.

Here is another tidbit of information to make your manifesting optimal. Many people seem to obsess when they start manifesting. I have had numerous clients—more than I can count—who are quite determined to manifest everything they want. This is great. But, they seem to think that if they say their whole manifest script ten times a day or more than once a week, they can make everything happen sooner. This is obsession. Obsessing is negative and fear-based. Positive energy brings positive energy; keep the balance and keep the energy exchange.

Please *just* follow the directions for manifesting. Manifest once a week with true intent. Know it will happen and *know that you deserve the manifest.* Trust and believe.

Meditating to Connect with Self

I'm going to explain more on how you can connect. You can blissfully connect all of you in one meditation. Hey, *no* overthinking right now; just read this before your brain starts telling you you can't. Everyone can. Let's get you to master self-connection first.

There are words people use to describe meditation to connect with yourself. Some call this a connection to your Akashic records. (The Akashic records are a library, a place to tap into to see your life's path. Some people believe everything is set in stone or in this library on another dimension. It is filled with books and/or information about what is or can happen in your life.) I like to call it the *all-knowing you* or *your higher self* meditation. I say this because it comes from *you;* you are drawing sensations—positive vibrations, visions, and energy—to do this particular meditation. It is your *inner knowing* that you are tapping into. It is not a black hole or anything like that. Self-connection is the most beautiful connection. It's almost indescribable because it can feel unreal that you are so incredibly smart, loving, understanding, and kind!

A few times in my connection meditation with my higher self, I had knowledge of some subjects that I previously had never known about. It is enlightening to know that the inner me is extremely "worldly." It's like my *go-to* buddy when I'm in a predicament, or when I just need to breathe and understand what is the best action for me to move forward.

If you love the outdoors, as I do, *walking meditation* might be best for you. This brings high vibes and is great exercise, too. I start by putting my walking shoes on, then I head outside my home, and I state that *I am walking to release, relax, and give thanks.* I do a one-mile walk forward and a one-mile walk back home. On the walk forward, with my inner voice, I name who and what I am thankful for in my life and why. I include people, the air I breathe, the water I drink, the food I eat, and every animal, bug, and living thing. I include the planets, the sun, the moon, the earth, and myself. I appreciate nature and its beauty as I walk. I smile, as I am grateful for my legs, my eyes, and all my functioning body parts, inside and out. I give thanks to my spirit guides and universal source.

When I reach the turning point, I breathe in and out and continue back with manifesting thoughts for myself—what I desire and project to happen for myself and others. I keep only positive thoughts and visions and loving projections. When I arrive at my door, I am relaxed and on high vibes with all that goodness! Plus I had some good blood flow in my body from walking. After I drink some water, I am now ready to *connect*. I'm in such a great mood and have great energy—of course anyone would want to connect with me! Everyone loves to be around happy, high-vibe people! Especially my higher self. I created high vibrations at a frequency that is utmost positivity, that enables me to connect easily and effortlessly.

Only *you* can prevent the connection. If you are afraid to connect to yourself, that will prevent it. A common reason is that you don't want to change or may be afraid of change. I can share that only positive change can come of your true connection. It is not about any type of religion or faith. This is truly about your connection with the part of you that is unconditional love and about the ability of sensing what is best for you.

I connect to my higher self at least twice a week, but only in meditation. I don't necessarily disconnect, but I set the intention and opening (this is what you desire and project) that I am "listening" to my higher self's advice at all times. Then, once I have done my meditation connection session, I give myself gratitude and let myself know I am ready to start my day.

Meditating to Connect with Archangels

Back in the day, when I started receiving clairaudient messages and noticing all my gifts of ESP, I would hear and sense an energy around me sharing really nice messages and guiding me. Finally, I realized he wanted to help me and advise me in positive ways. I said, "Hi, I'm sure you know my name is Jolie already, but may I ask what is yours?"

I heard a male voice say, "Michael."

I said, "Hello and thank you for all you are helping me with. I appreciate you." At the time, I had no clue about archangels or ascended masters, because I was self-taught with my intuitive abilities.

Now just so you know, Archangels are everyone's angels, not just mine or yours. They are here for the greater good of humanity and want all of us to be the best we can for ourselves, each other, and the earth. After all, this is what keeps universal energy flowing and harmonious. Each one of us counts in this big cosmic universe! So when you are not happy, you affect others, and so on and so forth.

The term *calling in* is basically asking for a god, goddess, archangel, ascended master—anything other than a human—to come join you in a conversation, in a meditation, or just to pal around. It's best to call them in when you really need them, because they are busy. As they are multidimensional beings, they can be in more than one place at once (obviously, because most of us call on God quite often, and he sure handles a lot of calls at once). The same goes for the rest of the super light team of the universe. They are happy to come, especially if the visit will help you become your absolute best self.

Here are fourteen famous archangels and what they are known for:

1. *Archangel Michael*—He is powerful and strong. Michael is my number one archangel. I love asking him to connect with me; he is very direct and to the point with his energy. He brings protection and releases all fears and negativity in any space, including your "headspace." He helps with personal power and elevates psychic power as well. He is loving but blunt, and he speaks with honor, truth, and love. He respects all and teaches all to be respectful. One word to describe him is protector. You may notice bright white, royal blue, or gold if you call him in for a meditation.

2. *Archangel Raphael*—He is known for a green, light presence, green representing healing of all levels: physical, emotional, mental, and spiritual. He helps other healers in their practices by becoming energy that advances one's healing abilities and notions. He can bring vibrations to adjust all wounds—past, present, or future. His

description is "healer." The color you may notice if you call him in for a meditation is brilliant green. He is my go-to for physical healing for clients. I humbly ask for his frequencies to flow through my body to another person's to assist them in the healing process. Being a conduit for elevated beings is like receiving gratitude and giving gratitude—a perfect energy exchange. It sometimes leaves me speechless; the experience is so beautiful.

3. *Archangel Ariel*—She works with nature and animals. She is considered the guardian and healer of animals. Hmm, aren't we animals, too? One word to describe her is *strength*. The color you may notice if you call Ariel in for a meditation is pale pink or shades of hot pink. When she arrives, I instantly feel my feet connect to Earth. I submit to the elemental energy she provides.

4. *Archangel Gabriel*—Gabriel is known for being the communicator of God. Through writing, art—all types of expression, including messages that come through animals and earthly means. The best description of Gabriel is "messenger." The color you may notice if you call Gabriel in for a meditation is bold copper or gold. When I was younger, I didn't know much about angels. As I reached my thirties, I was lucky enough to be visited by angels and to learn about them and their mystical energy. Unknowingly, when I performed readings, I would channel the words *I am just a channel, a messenger*. Archangel Gabriel taught me that these were not my messages, but Archangel Michael's words and visions that channeled through me, a *messenger of the light*. I was taught how to sharpen my intuitive abilities with Archangel Gabriel and many of the angels. I downloaded ways to be best at my calling and purpose. Most importantly, I learned from Gabriel that we all can be messengers, but we have to be accurate listeners.

5. *Archangel Chamuel*—He helps with relationships, romantic and otherwise. He brings higher vibrations so humans can attract the right connections for friendships and love relationships. One word to

describe him: *relationships*. The color you may notice if you call him in for a meditation is pale green to chartreuse.

6. *Archangel Azrael*—He is the angel of death, but death is also known as rebirthing. He comforts families that endure loss and brings loving, calming energy to those in need, providing compassion and a knowing that their loved ones have crossed into the light. A one-word description: *calming*. The color you may notice if you call him in for a meditation is pale yellow to cream. You can ask him to assist you in your meditation to connect with those who have passed over into the light.

7. *Archangel Haniel*—He enhances spiritual power and connectivity to the divine. He helps us with our senses and abilities, such as psychic intuition. He helps us with grace and love. One word to describe him is *expansion*. The colors you may notice if you call him in for a meditation are deep blue and white. As you meditate and learn to open your third eye, you may feel the presence of Archangel Haniel within your inner mind.

8. *Archangel Jeremiel*—He is the angel of hope. He is an activist, helping those who need to pass over into the light and find the correct dimension. He provides love and compassion without judgment. He can help you wake up and see what is needed to adapt to change in your life. He can help you resolve issues in your current life. The color you may notice if you call him in for a meditation is a deep purple or violet.

9. *Archangel Jophiel*—She helps us when we need to feel structured and secure. She brings confidence and agility to provide you with what you need inside your mind to move ahead and be strong. Best words for her: *self-esteem builder*. The color you may notice if you call her in for a meditation is candy-apple red. When Jophiel visits, your senses will be heightened, and mental colors and imagery become almost realistic.

10. *Archangel Metatron*—He brings focus and motivation and relieves stress in one's life. They say he was once human and that is why he relates to us more than another angels. Archangel Metatron is a twin of Archangel Sandalphon. He helps with reaching goals and achievements that are important to you. The colors you may notice if you call him in for a meditation are light green and mystical violet. It is common when he visits to feel or sense and sometimes see geometric shapes within your inner mind. It can feel psychedelic. When this occurs, feelings of power emerge from your being. Hold a geometric crystal while calling Archangel Metatron to your meditation session, and sensational vibrations become inspirational messages. You can use amethyst in a pyramid shape to bring in plenty of insightful and soothing energy. I enjoy holding a clear quartz to get new perspectives when I feel stuck in my thoughts. It kicks me into newness and brilliant ideas.

11. *Archangel Raziel*—He brings us a strong bond with self and spirit. He brings you to know your inner truth and to keep your faith in positive outlooks of life. The best phrase to describe him is "teacher of self-love." The colors you may notice if you call him in for a meditation are all the colors of the rainbow! I relate rainbow colors to success. I have seen countless rainbows in my self-awareness meditations; take twenty minutes and see yours!

12. *Archangel Sandalphon*—He is known to be the link between man and spirit. He is the twin of Archangel Metatron, who also was once human on Earth before ascending to the light. He is a listener more than anything; he listens to all humans' prayers and brings the messages to the universe to be heard and answered. The best word to describe him is *listener*. The color you may notice if you call him in for a meditation is powerful turquoise.

13. *Archangel Uriel*—He brings us enlightenment to have us reveal our own strengths and weaknesses to become better. He empowers you and helps you strengthen your soul. He helps you speak to

your higher self, the part of you that is there to tap into for guidance and love. The color you may notice if you call him in for a meditation is a beautiful, bright yellow.

14. *Archangel Zadkiel*—He is inspirational and encourages us to love ourselves and others. He reminds us of our past lessons and to notice the present. He helps with forgiveness and heals old wounds emotionally and mentally. He wants you to be righteous in loving actions. The colors you may notice if you call him in for a meditation are hues of purple and deep indigo.

Meditating to Connect with Ascended Masters

Now that you have the details on the archangels, here are two of my favorite ascended masters to meditate with. Ascended masters were once human on Earth and have ascended, transforming into the light. They are and will always be recognized for their good doings for the world.

1. *Saint Germaine*—Saint Germaine is considered the king of alchemy. He was said to have made healing tinctures with herbs and flowers. He healed others in his time. Some people believe he is the lord of the seventh dimension—the highest dimension. He is also called "the freedom fighter," as he had to hide his abilities during his time (he was telepathic, could levitate, and was capable of astral transport). The color I sense during a meditation with Saint Germaine is violet with gold. This vision may be a sign of the violet flame, which represents love, healing, and freedom.

2. *Galileo Galilei*—He was and is a brilliant mathematician, astrologer, and physicist. He produced writings about the planets, stars, and their movement. He was a teacher of many subjects, such as using pendulums as a clock. I love to ask Galileo to come into my meditation because he loves to share his knowledge of philology and has amazing perspectives of people, the cosmos, and the earth. You will feel as if you have downloaded the smarts!

I often ask for assistance from several different energies while meditating, and one is the famous Galileo. I heard him quite often as I first asked about some cosmic events and how they affect us. Believe it or not, I was his scribe in the old days. I was asking about rebirth and if I could calculate a new life from our star. I had a few astrologers look into my birth date and Galileo's time and location, and apparently it was quite possible we could have been in the same dimensional time frame. What an honor. A quick meditation with Galileo can look like this: Grab an ocean jasper stone, as it brings good communication with spirit, balances all the chakras, and ignites your visual imagery. Hold it with your left hand, preferably outdoors in the night air if stars are abundant. Ask Galileo to teach you something about the planets. Sit with patience—you may have an empowering thought or two. A true sign of his presence can be that wisdom or something science-y! Don't forget to give him gratitude for showing up and schooling you.

Please feel free to call upon one of these incredible beings of light to assist you in your meditations. I suggest calling in just one at a time; if you are feeling and receiving, it can get confusing with multiple messages all at once. If you call one in and you don't feel they are there, they most certainly are, so just know they are listening to your needs and requests. Sometimes silence is incredible and just as strong.

These beings are of the light, meaning that they are of the highest vibrational frequency: unconditional love. This unquestionably is the best feeling you can ever encounter.

Guided Meditation versus On-the-Fly Meditation

We've begun to discuss how to meditate on your own. But I'd also like to suggest you try guided meditations. I have found that there are guided meditations (recorded meditations) for every style and purpose.

The biggest factor in choosing to use guided meditations is your mood at that point in time. I personally love guided meditations when I want to do my journey or connect with my guides. Guided meditations quickly take me to my bliss; sometimes they take me to a past life across space, or I'll be guided to a beautiful space near the ocean or in a field of flowers. If I can resonate with the person's voice in a guided meditation, they can get me to my bliss.

I always love to try new guided meditations. As you change and shift in life, so can your tastes in what you like. The most important consideration of doing a guided meditation instead of doing one on your own is making sure you feel safe and comfortable in your space and that you can get to your bliss. I offer a few guided meditations on my website Crystaljunkie.com that you can download. You can also record yourself reading the meditations you are drawn to to make your own guided meditation.

Whether guided, group, or on the fly, meditation can get you to a higher vibration. You would be smart to pick meditations that resonate with you and your intention, opening, or purpose at that particular time. The more you practice or enjoy a blissful state of mind, the easier it is to reach bliss.

We are starting with meditation with the self, then moving to a fabulous meditation with your higher self. I have also included instructions on autowriting in chapter 7. Then, we can take steps to place you in nature or have vivid, wild mind travels. I call these journeys of the mind.

The next way of meditation is optional for those of you who are comfortable with connecting to those who have passed over into the light. This connection can be very beautiful. If this isn't your cup of tea, beeline to connecting with your source, such as a deity, an archangel, or other amazing beings of light. It's really fun to have a telepathic buddy from the light.

Moon Cycle Meditations

The moon goes through many cycles. It is common to hear of the new moon and the full moon, but there are other phases of the moon's cycle in the sky. There is the first quarter, which is just a sector of the moon's phase, and the third quarter, which is another sector of the moon's phase. A supermoon is when the moon is closest to Earth, and a micromoon is when it is farthest away.

A new moon usually makes people feel as if they are in a starting stage. This is a good time to set short-term goals—a weekly movement forward for self. Some people believe that a full moon is a completion of a cycle. I get that, but isn't every ending a new beginning? That's my take on it, so we can feel one way or another about this fine cosmic day of the month. During a full moon, I manifest new things and give thanks for what I have already accomplished, allowing those frequencies, lessons, and experiences to educate me to become a higher being on Earth.

A blue moon is when there are two full moons in one three-day cycle. Two full moons in one month is rare, but it happens. It is a powerful time felt by many people as an energetic shifting of their souls. A blue moon cycle is a really strong time to connect with yourself.

I have noticed that when there is a supermoon or a micromoon, there is an opposite effect of what we visually see in the sky. Many people seem to be more chaotic or anxious during these moon phases, but it is also the best and greatest time energetically to manifest your desires and goals with conviction. The frequencies are amplified, making the outcome stronger and more vibrant. It seems the subconscious really hears and connects with what you are desiring and asking for because of the moon's amplification.

When our conscious and subconscious align in the same frequency, we can accomplish or manifest stronger and faster because of the unity connection of self on a soul level. All of you that exists connects, and that, I believe, is one of the strongest energies on Earth. As you get ready to ascend, this next chapter offers the five methods of meditation: nonactive–slightly awake, active-awake, active physical body movement, mindful thoughts, and—my favorite—meditation without thoughts, also known as mindless meditation.

Chapter 2
The Five Methods of Meditation

Knowing what you want to instill or receive with a meditation is just as important as the meditation process. Meditating is perfectly intriguing, eye-opening, and insightful. You will find the five methods are for everyone to adapt. By the way, did I mention that meditation *rocks*!

Nonactive–slightly awake, active-awake, active physical body movement, mindful thoughts, and meditation without thoughts are the five methods. I teach my students to try all five because one method can resonate better than others, since we all have different lifestyles and time limitations.

Nonactive–Slightly Awake Meditation

This meditation uses all your senses in a completely relaxed conscious and subconscious state. This meditation practice can connect you to your higher self or soul.

Have you ever woken from your sleep feeling super unbalanced? Try this. Get your mind to a positive balance with a visualization or by "creating." Creating is relaxing and feeling something that you want to enhance. It changes your frequency as you visualize your thoughts or activities for that day. I imagine myself having a wonderful day before I wake up, and sometimes I go through my daily duties. Everything then moves super smoothly, making my day easy and fun. If I feel any pains in my physical body before I wake, I imagine that part of my body feeling perfectly well. I imagine all my cells moving to that part and healing it. I imagine wonderful white light washing over that part of my body, and anything negative is gone; I only replace it with positive healing light, allowing me to feel perfectly well.

An easy way to track the benefits of meditation is to keep a record of feelings before and after the session. In the last chapter, I presented an exercise to identify your current frequency on a scale of one to ten and to choose certain meditations to raise your frequency. This is a different idea. This scale is to show yourself you can relax your body within a few energy breaths. It is about giving yourself permission using breathing. To do this, use a scale of one to five (one means low vibrations, five means high vibrations). Let's start with your current frequency. Are you feeling a two? Maybe a four? Write it down. To create an adjustment of your energy, sit in a comfortable chair. Gently close your eyes. Inhale one long breath in, and release that breath as slowly as you can. Breathe in and exhale slowly a total of three times. Now, open your eyes.

What frequency number are you now? You should be at least one number higher. If you didn't raise the number, say aloud, "I allow myself to completely relax." Then continue the breath work a few more times. This will improve your frequency, making you calmer, more relaxed. Keep up with the breath work until you are feeling a four or five. This is the easiest way to adjust your frequency and successfully complete a nonactive–slightly awake meditation.

Active-Awake Meditation

A practice that instills peace while being aware and mindful of one's senses. This meditation is basically a mindful awareness of your senses as you are conscious and effortlessly noticing what you experience. A few examples would be doing a session of exercise or restorative yoga. Active-awake meditations can be done virtually anywhere. You can do this method with a person guiding you or completely solo, indoors or out. One of my favorites is with a small group of six or less where everyone is sitting. There is one professional meditation instructor taking all of us through a journey that connects with all our senses through thought storytelling. We imagine and create an atmosphere in our minds to feel fresh grass beneath our feet as a huge ceremonial fire is burning and large drums are being played. That is just a taste of what your active meditation could be.

I have a secret about this particular active-awake meditation method. If you use your imagination, you can create detailed visualizations in your mind, just like a painter or artist. Start by imagining one color. For example, a light sky blue. Your eyes can be opened or closed—whatever is most comfortable. Let's make the light blue a triangle. Now, make that light blue triangle the size of a piece of pizza. Now, this slice of pizza has some toppings: vegetables, cheeses, meats—whatever you desire. Imagine all the toppings you want on it. The next step is noticing how it may smell to you. Take a few moments to taste that pizza. If you are able to do at least part of this mini method, you have successfully activated all of your six senses. If it was a bit challenging for you or maybe you are not a pizza fan, try to bring your focus to something other than food and bring in all your senses to really connect with it. This is an active-awake meditation. This method can make you a master of meditation in no time.

Active Physical Body Movement Meditation

Full awareness of your senses using your physical body and actions. This could be cooking, running, driving, walking, golfing, and so on. It is performing an action without mindful thinking. It is activity and going through motions while forgetting about time. Remember, you can be on autopilot doing the actions as your mind goes to mind space. An example is runner's high—doing without thinking. Active physical body movement meditation can be mindful, also; focus, be creative with imagery, or use the meditation to mindfully manifest. See how you can create crossover combinations of the five methods of meditation.

Meditation with Mindful Thoughts

This is concentrating and noticing with ease as you are using all your senses. It can be a journey or visualization of an exotic place or creative journey. One method I relate strongly to is meditation with rosary beads or a mala.

Prayer is considered, in my book, to be a cognitive-mindful-awake meditation. When you pray, you are sending something or a person wishes or thoughts of goodness or health. This is what I call a "thought form" vibration. Any positive thought for someone or something is a positive thought form of energy vibrations. The high positive vibrations move over space and time to that person or persons on Earth or wherever they may be, including other dimensions like heaven, or whatever you believe in. Sending positive thoughts and love is powerful.

Since everything we say or think is a vibration—a frequency—you can understand that what you are administering is a constructive positive energy directed at that specific person, animal, or place. For example, if I was setting my intention and opening to do a prayer specifically to express love to my grandmother, who has passed into the light, I would sit or lie down and focus my thoughts on something positive and loving I remember about her, like her making me a sandwich without the crust. She said if I ate the crust, my hair would get tangled! That thought makes me smile and laugh. I am on high vibrations now, and I say, "Grandma, I love you. Thank you for being here for me back then and now. I love you. I know you are in a beautiful place and want you to know that I miss and love you."

Manifesting is also considered meditation with mindful thoughts, since you are undeniably placing positive intent and energy exchanges to create a vibrational frequency, your frequency going out to the universe to bring opportunity of what you desire to occur.

There are so many phenomenal ways you can be mindful while meditating. Another is noticing the colors in the rainbow, which correlate to the human chakras, then creating a noun that represents each color. For example, green can be a tree, red can be a stop sign, blue can be your bedroom wall, and so on. You can customize these nouns and colors to your life, which makes it more fun. Occasionally, when I overthink, I do the color-noun thing, and as I am in one room, I only allow myself to use all items within that certain location. This is cool to do outdoors in nature as well.

Meditation without Thoughts

Mindless meditation is when you forget about time. Yep. Place that cell phone and clock far, far away. *Time* is what keeps us thinking. It makes us think of *what* we should do, *how* we should do it, and *where* and *when* we should do it. It also makes us feel that certain places and things need to be categorized. On top of all that thinking, you are trying to decide if you really want to do all those tasks or not!

No wonder your mind is so active! Busy, busy, busy. Sometimes our minds are busier than our bodies while doing these actions. A hamster wheel comes to my mind. Overthinking can be a drag. Round and round you go—just stop that thought, and let it go! Meditation without thoughts is skipping the middleman of actions: time.

Get a notepad and a pen. Write down those things that are in your head—those thoughts that are going round and round like a hamster wheel. I know, I know; you say you cannot stop thinking of them, because if you do, you will forget to do all those things, and some of it is work that you get paid to do.

Yeah, yeah, I heard that before. Just do it. No excuses. Write the things down and get your thoughts on paper. Mindless meditation creates subconscious bliss where you have allowed yourself to travel outside the bodily form. This could be astral projection to a past or parallel life, an alternate universe or dimension visit, or simply a daydream!

I have stared up at the clouds in the sky while lying flat on the ground outdoors to allow mindlessness. At first, I would see shapes form in the clouds; sometimes they would look like animals or angel wings. The wind would slowly move the clouds. I hit mindlessness, Zen, once I let go of wondering if the cloud was a shape of something. This meditation just required me to relax; I let go of visual connection to just notice without thoughts.

Another way to reach mindlessness is to start doing breath work. Deep breathing in, and exhaling out strong so you can hear your breath leaving your body—do this six times. It is best to be sitting comfortably or lying down. Inside or outside is fine, as long as you are in a safe environment. After the breath work, think of the color white and imagine everything is white around you; you can get lost in that light, and nothing but feeling comes through—just white light. The thoughts of white and feeling the light eventually bring you to a mindless state. I find this method is best on a day when you are not restricted by time. It would be perfect if you had a day off or a vacation when trying this meditation. People always seem to reach mindless meditation easier when the thought of time is not on their radar. I have noticed that people who have an easier time with this type of meditation are more at ease in their current life and are usually not the worrying type. Either way, you can train yourself to be blissful in mind space—after all, it takes practice to go nowhere!

———

Meditation has a variety of methods, but I simplify how to use each method to suit your personal needs. There are many reasons why you may want to incorporate this amazing habit into your life. It's cool to know you can switch it up so you never get bored. You can always hit another high frequency to specifically change the experience of a meditation.

Note that you will receive multiple examples of each method throughout this book. There is no limit. Knowing you can pull out this book and hit an easy meditation for five minutes or more totally rocks. Oh, it gets good. Actually, fantastic. Just give yourself five minutes or more a day and allow yourself to connect or meditate for a good purpose.

Chapter 3
Tools to Help Boost Meditation

There are lots of tools you can use to create those high-frequency energies to ramp up your meditations. My favorites are crystals—well, you knew I was going to bring that up! I'll discuss crystals in part 2. First, let's look at some other tools, including crystal singing bowls, Tibetan metal singing bowls, a labyrinth spiral, mandalas, sacred geometry, and voiced mantras.

I like to use a combination of these. I start with a high vibrational frequency, meaning I get myself prepped to be happier than I currently am. Then, I choose my tool for my meditation.

When I explain that meditation and adding meditation tools raise your frequency, it doesn't mean they make you hyper. You can have a high frequency without being hyper, wired, nervous, jumpy, or overactive. Some people associate the word *high* with faster. Meditation raises your vibrational frequency for a better connection to self and your source. It can make you feel elated and euphoric. That is a healthy high. Meditation brings balance and overall wellness. Many of these tools raise your vibrations because they create additional vibrations from the energy they hold or emit from their makeup. Therefore, adding that tool's frequency to your current frequency raises you up that much higher. Remember, you can gauge your frequency before and after your meditations to see the difference!

If I am indoors, it's important to have a clean space, which means less clutter and more openness with a bit of light. My first tool is usually my crystal bowl. I play it for a few minutes and say a few loving mantra messages to myself, such as, "I am 100 percent capable in all I set my mind to. I am good, loving, and kind." I say this aloud or sometimes in my head. Then I set my water diffuser with some lavender or bergamot essential oil and dab some oil on my wrist. I grab my high-vibe crystals that synergize with my purposeful meditation and begin my intention and opening.

Most of us feel it is important to declutter and clean our space. It can make it easier to think and brings vibrant energy to any space. To change the vibe within your home or office, try this frequency raiser. First, pick a crystal from your collection that calls out to you. Just look at all your crystals and pick up the ones that attract you. Then state aloud, "I am 100 percent capable in all I set my mind to. I am good, loving, and kind." If you have any essential oils, dab a bit of your favorite on your wrist, then start a purposeful meditation and begin your intention and opening.

If you are outdoors, you can walk a homemade rock labyrinth, smell the fresh air, and open your senses. If you don't do the meditation walk or labyrinth, sit with your back against your favorite tree trunk. Then take several deep breaths in and out in the fresh air. Take a few moments to listen to the birds and the leaves of the trees while looking at a flower or something planted in your yard. Enjoy the feeling of the breeze or sun on your skin. This all can make you feel comfy and ready to connect.

Now, let's take a look at each of these tools.

Crystal or Tibetan Singing Bowls

Crystal or Tibetan singing bowls are some of the best sound tools. What is a singing bowl? It is a bowl made to emit sound vibrations you can hear that continue to resonate to keep a high frequency. The sound raises your frequency because it clears all the lower or stagnant frequencies from your aura layers and chakras and then balances your chakras. This clearing and balancing can occur simultaneously. The sound emitted can cleanse space, cleanse your aura, and align your chakras! It can also cleanse your crystals and anything that is within its vibrational reach. Singing bowls can be tuned for specific chakras or to all seven chakras. Crystal bowls and all high-frequency sound tools are useful in the acceleration of the human body healing itself. This healing sound travels through blood, bones, and muscles, which enables the healing process. This is also true of tuning forks that many holistic doctors use. I love the sounds that a crystal bowl gives off; the sound is so profound that you feel super enlightened after playing it.

Figure 3: Singing Bowls

A crystal singing bowl is made up of almost any type of crystal. Typically they are quartz, but I have heard and played ones that were made of moldavite and rose quartz, too. These crystals are shaped into bowls with a specific thickness and tuned to a certain vibrational frequency. These crystal bowls can be tuned to the frequency of any of the seven chakras.

You can play a crystal bowl by gently tapping a suede dowel against the bowl's top lip. This creates an incredible sound vibration that cleanses the space you are in, clears your aura, and balances your chakras. In five minutes, you are in a heavenly state.

The Tibetan bowls are different because they are made of metals. They play great, too, but it's apples and oranges as far as the sound, in my opinion. Both types of bowls come in a variety of sizes and composites depending on the player's preferences. Some practitioners travel for their performances, playing all seven chakra-tuned bowls to a meditative audience. If you have a chance to go to a local crystal singing bowl event, it's something you will remember and love. Events can be found usually at mindfulness centers, yoga studios, and metaphysical stores that offer classes. You can certainly purchase a bowl or a set for your daily meditative practice. I play all seven quite frequently, as that is one of my favorite classes to offer. The session gives you a sense of cleanliness from pushing all other lower vibrations out and away from you.

You can use any of these singing bowls in your own meditative practice. I find they are great tools to raise my frequency and clear my stagnant energy in minutes! Anytime you feel the need to lift your mood or adjust your frequency for the day, grab your crystal bowl and dowel and play, play, play!

Mandalas

In Sanskrit, the word *mandala* means circle, center, or sacred circle. Merriam-Webster defines it as a "symbol of the universe."[4] Carl Jung calls mandalas "archetypes of wholeness."[5] Historically, mandalas have been used as a communication tool to connect with God, the higher self, the inner self, or source.

Mandalas have been used in many countries since ancient times for healing and meditation. They hold and emit vibrations. Positive mandalas bring awareness and are great tools for meditations. There are some mandalas that are specifically created for certain uses, such as self-realization. Mandalas are sacred geometry and should be used with loving intentions.

Sacred geometry pictures, drawings, or paintings have shapes that are precise and usually symmetrical. I have found that perfect shapes are powerful to use in meditation, but I also did my own studies of imperfect shapes. These shapes also draw in powerful energy, keep my focus, and bring me a deeper connection to my inner knowing and self-realizations.

4. Merriam-Webster, "Mandala," https://www.merriam-webster.com/dictionary/mandala.

5. Carl Jung, *The Archetypes and The Collective Unconscious*, 2nd ed. (Princeton, NJ: Princeton University, 1980).

Figure 4: Mandala

I did my research by channeling paintings or energy art, which my guides from the light call mandalas or life shifters. The guides of light appear only to help humans have betterment and heal. They come to me in my channeling state of mind. It started when I would occasionally feel a calling to paint, which was brought on by these light beings. I would just go into a trance, start moving and gathering supplies, and then paint a wall, a linen, or anything in those moments.

This *doing* without full consciousness was a meditative state. It was also combined with higher spirit knowledge. The guides showed me that simply looking at the painting would change the frequency of my body. At the same time of painting, I would stop and autowrite the guides' messages of what exactly these paintings were supposed to do as far as adjusting our frequencies and using them as tools for meditation.

No matter the size or shape, if the mandalas are created with positive energy, they will emit positive energy. These channeled messages and guided paintings of mandalas are not all in perfect symmetry. I realize that some perfectly symmetrical symbols are indeed very powerful, and I love to use them in meditation, but I know my self-made—or should I say spirit-channeled—

mandalas are tools embedded with frequency symbols that can be slightly imperfect but boost positive charges.

During that time of painting the mandalas, I had an awakening. These guides shared that humans are not perfect, therefore the paintings that were channeled through me would adjust or balance my imperfections and those of other humans. Interesting how all energy can be powerful when it comes from a pure, loving source!

I ended up channeling more than forty-four mandalas from these healing spirit guides of light. All I created are now on the walls of my first retail metaphysical store in Boca Raton, Florida. People come from all over to gaze at them and feel their personalized vibes.

We often use the mandala paintings to do a self-reading. Once a visitor looks all of them over quickly, they point out the three they are most attracted to. We flip over the three and read the messages the guides provided regarding how to use those mandalas and what the viewer needs to shift in their lives. The messages always match what they need at that time in their life! It is eye-opening. I am grateful that I was gifted this ability to paint meaningful frequency art to share with people.

Soon, a woman said she would like to own one of the mandalas and work with it. She suggested not only prints but to make an oracle deck of them all. And so I did. They are sensational to meditate with. The meditation methods could be awake, slightly-awake, or mindless. The first two are obvious; however, you may be wondering how a mandala can work without thoughts. Art creates frequencies that can positively shift and balance your aura, even if you are not looking at it. Totally incredible!

Mandala Amplifiers

The guides then began to educate me through my clairaudient abilities that crystals were amplifiers. I could place certain crystals on top of the painted mandala to create more powerful meditations that would embed a positive frequency of energy into my electromagnetic fields. Those spirit guides were quite scientific!

They further showed me that adding essential oils could elevate a human's senses. This would be beneficial to use with hand mudras. Hand mudras involve placing your hands in specific positions and holding them over the mandala art. This accentuates the vibrations I feel from the mandala. It is quite an incredible experience, to say the least!

Flower of Life

The flower of life symbol is a geometric pattern that has six overlapping circles that are equal in radius and look two-dimensional. This famous pattern is in multiple historic artifacts ranging from the Roman Empire to Islamic art, gothic designs, and New Age items. The flower of life symbolizes creation, the unity of all that exists, and life force energy, which is chi or our energy. It shows us that everything runs through everything; all affects all. It is a repeating pattern that is evenly spread to infinite energy and life. It is believed that the repeated circles bring abundance. Some say it is the pattern of the universe, like a digital code of all that is.

Figure 5: Flower of Life

As a mandala, its sacred geometry enlightens my mind and brings in equality and neutral feelings when I feel unbalanced. When I am angered, it calms my mind and clears my auric fields. I have a necklace with the flower of life on it. The backside has the sacred geometry of Archangel Metatron's symbol. I can feel it before I place it on my body. I have to tell you, it is potent!

I noticed that when I wear it, other people walk up to me more than normal due to the attraction of the two symbols.

Let's have some fun with this and experiment. Wear any geometric symbol, mandala, or sacred geometry; it can be a crystal or a painted or printed item. Then see what attention you receive, the quality of the attention (hoping it's all positive), and, most importantly, how you feel while wearing the frequencies. This will be fun. I experimented several different ways by not just wearing these items in public, but in people's homes and offices and businesses to create the energy that vibed with their goals and purposes. Once you have had some fun with this, email me (Crystaljunkie@outlook.com). Meditating while holding the flower of life symbol is quite profound, and you may find yourself channeling or empowered with worldly views.

Labyrinths

A labyrinth is a spiral that represents a path of purpose. It is understanding the journey of our life moving into its center, our balance, then back out into the world as a new, whole, balanced person.

I have been to several sacred grounds where labyrinths are a featured space. Once you are there at the beginning of the spiral path, you follow its spirals inward. In the middle of the spiral, there is usually a space where people place notes, wishes, and prayers for self or for others. Then you travel back out, feeling grateful and hopeful, knowing your requests will be heard by the spiritual world. It can be quite an emotional experience.

Many public or shared labyrinths have lots of loving energy and prayer vibrations attached to them. That space is a spiral, a vortex of vibrational energy of thoughts and mindful emotions. Those are powerful intentions by many visitors.

I created a small labyrinth in my backyard, which is smaller than the places I visit at spiritual centers and enlightenment lodges. I placed stones to create a path I could walk, and at a center point, I placed multiple stones in a pile so it was noticeably the middle. Then, I continued the spiral outward. I perform an active walking meditation with my labyrinth that takes about eight minutes, unless I decide to sit in the center a bit for manifesting or giving thanks.

Figure 6: Labyrinth

After I leave the labyrinth, I feel so inspired, loved, and recharged. I strongly appreciate how lucky I am to have a life, to be happy, and to be able to change if I need to. It puts me in touch with my free will and power.

When making my labyrinth, my lawn helper kind of messed it up; they assumed it was just a pile of rocks. I decided to remake it, and it was just as powerful to create it once again with loving thoughts. I thought, possibly, just maybe, the universe wanted me to re-create the labyrinth with more love than the first time.

Mantras

A mantra is words you can repeat daily to help you stay aligned with positive vibrations. Verbalized mantras are powerful. I love using my voice for meditation.

One example of a mantra is this: "Meditation is simply relaxing. Only I can control me. I allow myself to relax. I can relax my mind and my body." Just say it for giggles. Here is another mantra to say: "I am important. I allow myself to relax my mind and body. I will remain important."

Another form of mantra is your voice repeating *ohm*, a universal sound of love and unity. This can bring your frequency super high, especially prior to meditation. I was intuitively taught by the light beings to verbalize *oh lah me oh lahhh* at least three times. They taught me that this mantra creates an energy vortex that clears anything other than good from you or your space. It is also potent as a protection mantra. Two in one; you've got to love that.

There are mantras that are tuned to the chakras. These vowel sounds activate our body's energy and bring us to a high vibration. Here are the chakras with coordinating vowels, colors, notes, and hertz (Hz) frequencies. I made you a little chart to practice.

Chakra Mantras

Chakra	Vowel	Color	Note	Hz Frequency
Crown	EEE	violet, white, or gold	B	963
Third Eye	AYE	indigo blue	A	852
Throat	EYE	light blue	G	741
Heart	AH	green or pink	F	639
Solar Plexus	OH	yellow	E	528
Sacral	OOO	orange	D	417
Base Root	UH	red	C	396

A meditation exercise using mantras that I like to do is called "a relaxing test of feeling *thyself*." I start by sitting comfortably and saying certain words to myself. For instance, I say aloud, "Love." Then I say internally, "Love." These words give me a wide variety of emotions.

You can repeat them a few times and feel as if your body is getting lighter. I really feel that good vibe energy! You are raising your physical and energetic bodies' vibration. It makes me feel elated or as if I am escalating my energy.

This means my physical body and my energy body and aura are on a higher frequency, which just means good!

When I say the word in the inner mind, it is a vibration. Then, when I say the word out loud, I feel balanced. I am balanced inside and out! I do this all in one fifteen-minute sitting. If you forget about the words after you start, just keep feeling and *unthinking*. Feel free to forget about time as well. It is great!

You can say the words slowly or quickly. Repeat them a few times each and see how your energy feels afterward. Here are more words I say inwardly and outwardly:

- Beautiful
- Gratitude
- Happy
- Healthy
- Laughter
- Love

You might *feel* some of these words stronger than others as you say them aloud or within. Now, try to connect to each part of your body. You can also just pick a section of your body you find easiest to focus on. As you express the words, notice again each different section of your physical body. You will notice where in your body you feel the most. For example, when I say the word *laughter* in my mind, then aloud, I feel it in my throat area the most. Take a mental note of where you feel the word. It can be very telling of what is going on with you and in your life.

If you want to do a short test, say a positive word and notice your tone. Now say a negative word and notice your tone. Your frequency is created from the intent of the word and its meaning and tone. You should be able to clearly distinguish between them. That is why you may have learned early in life to watch what you say, or change your tone.

Sacred Geometry

Sacred geometry is the symbolism and meaning of shapes, and according to ancient scriptures, it promotes spirituality. Everything that exists is sacred geometry, from our atoms and DNA to every flower, rock, and animal. Sacred geometry is the mathematical equation that makes up the universe and beyond.

Geometric shapes can be drawn on paper, painted, imagined in your mind, written in the air with your hand, and, of course, made of crystals! They are powerful universal shapes. Here are some sacred geometry shapes and what they represent.

Tetrahedron

The tetrahedron is a three-dimensional symbol for balance and stability. No matter how you hold it, it keeps natural elemental balance between your body and spirit. This reminds me of the yin-yang symbol. Balance and love within self and your surroundings. Tetrahedrons are basically pyramids, and we all know how powerful they can be! Some believe they are connectors for extra-terrestrial communications.

Merkaba

The merkaba is a really interesting shape. It is one of the most powerful symbols because it is two star tetrahedrons combined. The ancients believed that the merkaba was the tool to communicate with heaven and the divine energies of existence. In Hebrew, *mer* means "light," *ka* means "spirit," and *ba* means "body."[6] Some also believe that one of the tetrahedron stars aligns with the stars and the other connects to Earth. In the Bible, the merkaba is mentioned and listed in the Old Testament forty-four times. The number forty-four in numerology brings success, healing, and enlightenment of the consciousness—a master number that equals the number eight. Eight is considered infinite energy and everlasting existence. A merkaba is truly a beautiful tool to meditate with. A merkaba made out of a quartz crystal is out of this world for telepathic communication with other people or with higher realms. If you love archangels, Archangel Metatron is the one who brings the power of all life with his connection and frequencies.

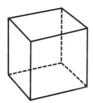

Hexahedron

The hexahedron is a cube-shaped, three-dimensional symbol. This is about grounding—being in the present moment and focused. It connects your energy to Earth, especially to nature. It correlates with nature's elements for grounding and the root chakra, helping us feel comfortable in our home called Earth!

6. Ancient-Symbols.com, "Merkaba Symbol," https://www.ancient-symbols.com/symbols -directory/merkaba.html.

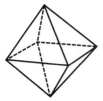

Octahedron

Octahedron is also three-dimensional and is often called the symbol of air. It is about love and compassion, breath and life. This shape helps you attune to self-love.

Icosahedron

Icosahedron is also a three-dimensional shape that brings fluidity of the creative self. It works with the element of water, which brings freedom and flow. Meditation with an icosahedron releases blockages and brings newness.

Dodecahedron

The dodecahedron is three-dimensional also! This symbol represents spirit, connecting with all our chakras. It is the element of ether, and it is perfect for reconnecting your earthly body to the light and higher realms.

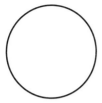

Sphere

The sphere is a simplistic shape; it is perfectly round and symbolizes completeness and equality. They say it holds wisdom of all the universe. Our cells, planets, and the sun are spheres—powerful and complete.

If you haven't tried a meditation with a drawn circle around your entire body, I am here to illuminate your aura! Let's perform this sphere meditation for positive health. Grab a carnelian and a bloodstone crystal to place in your hands or within the circle you are going to draw around your whole body. I suggest drawing the circle in sand or dirt. You can be creative and use a string or piece of material if you are indoors. The circle should be just big enough for you to sit inside it.

Once you make the circle, sit inside it and have the two crystals within the space. Now, visualizing each body part or organ one by one, say in your inner voice, "My heart is perfectly well and fine, perfectly functioning for a healthy human being on Earth." Take your time naming each part of your body and create positive frequencies by saying how well each is functioning.

If you want to go extra deep into this type of meditation, you can get a flash card deck of the human body. These decks can teach you what each organ, joint, or muscle is supposed to look like and how they function. Use those to make statements for positive health. Yes, I do have these flash cards. I use them quite often to repair my body! Just a reminder: the crystals are amplifiers and adjusters for this meditation. Carnelian helps blood flow and creative thoughts; bloodstone assists with blood disorders and creates physical strength, courage, and success.

You can create geometric shapes that you like best, then make a meditation that caters to your needs. You can add the shape to any meditation on the list. One of my monthly meditations is connecting with those who have passed over by using a triangle around my body. I make the shape from items I think the person would like: fresh flowers, something they gifted me, pieces of jewelry, and so on. I sometimes add a picture of them. Once you are set up and sitting within the shape, you can ask the person by name to visit you.

If you are a nature person like me, try this shape meditation. When I want to bring in more self-appreciation and gratitude to the earth, I go all out. I grab items that are meaningful to me. I grab my favorite crystals (cavansite and auralite 23), a few books I love, and I head outdoors. I make a four-foot circumference using anything I find in my yard—sticks, rocks, feathers, my dog. I am serious! My dog loves to sit near me in meditation; she has great vibes, and I love her. The arrangement is powerful. I settle myself within my item-based circle. I sit and feel each item as I create thoughts of thankfulness that I can touch, see, smell, and love all the items in my circle and those beyond my circle in nature. This twenty-minute bliss session really shifts my energy to extreme happiness.

Malas

Mala beads were and are used in Buddhism and Hinduism for meditation. Traditionally, people call them "prayer beads," similar to Catholic rosary beads. Each bead is held while a mantra is said, then you move to the next bead, and so on until you reach the last bead. A mala can be strung with gemstones—such as amethyst, rose quartz, or tiger's eye—or seeds, such as lotus, bodhi, rudraksha, Buddha nut, and rattan.

There are 108 beads on a mala.[7] The number 108 represents the 108 sacred places in the human body. Some believe it was the ancient Sanskrit scriptures that suggested 108, as it was the number of chapters in the yoga philosophy. The number fifty-four was also acknowledged as a "good" number of beads

7. Kate Vogt, *Mala of the Heart: 108 Sacred Poems* (New World Library, 2015).

in a mala since it is half of 108. Malas can have any amount of beads, but 108 and fifty-four are the most common, powerful, and mystical.

Math was never my best subject, but I directly resonate with wearing or holding a mala in the Slow Your Roll meditation (see chapter 8). I realized this was a quick way to slow my mind down and be mindful of my feelings and senses. This meditation really helped with my dyslexia. I can't believe I just labeled myself, but I want to share this because I know a lot of people out there struggle with this, too. In the Slow Your Roll with a Mala meditation, you use your concentrative mind and your senses with ease. It just happens. You don't have to try.

Now that you know what can add to your meditation, try each tool. It is very enjoyable to check out what you might sense differently from using each one. Now, let's move to my favorite tool of all: crystals.

Part 2

Using Crystals during Meditation

Chapter 4
How Crystals Work

Well, this is just my all-time favorite chapter! Did you know I am in love with crystals and their energies? It is undeniable that my favorite tools are crystals! Crystals come in all shapes and sizes. There are different classifications of crystals just as there are different crystal qualities. When using a crystal for meditation, the vibrational frequency will be emitted and start penetrating the aura layers of your energetic fields.

I previously wrote a book named *High-Vibe Crystal Healing*. It's full of crystal knowledge and tips for how to become an expert crystal healer at home or for professional use. Crystal layouts are self-healing techniques that can be used by everyone. It's a great reference book for finding a crystal remedy for most ailments.

Crystal healing can help you adjust your body's overall energy vibrations. There is a whole methodology of crystal healing, which is the knowledge and placement of crystals, minerals, and gemstones. Certain crystals laid on or off the body synergize with the person's energy vibrations to help them self-heal with releases and balance for wellness and advancement on a physical, emotional, mental, or spiritual level.

Crystals hold frequencies just like your body. Because of their makeup, certain crystals consist of elements that are healing. These elements have mineral content similar to vitamins that adjusts the body's energy and electromagnetic field. For example, minerals like magnesium or lithium can be in certain crystal compositions. Magnesium is a nutrient for the body; we actually need it to stay healthy. It regulates your muscles and nerve functions, balances blood sugar levels and blood pressure, and helps produce protein, bone, and DNA! Stones that contain magnesium vibrate at a frequency that can be healing to us on an energetic level through our aura layers and chakras, adjusting the frequencies as needed. (Please do not eat stones, of course.)

Lithium is a formation of quartz, but it also is included in other crystals and gemstones. A super popular stone called lepidolite has mica and large amounts of lithium within its structure. It is a light purple or gray color. Sometimes you can see little flecks of silver within it; that is the mica. Lithium is known for being used in the pharmaceutical drug Prozac, a mood balancer and stabilizer. As a crystal healer, I use lepidolite or lithium quartz in my clients' energy fields to balance their energy and correct their frequencies. If they are still in need of stability, many clients wear a lithium quartz or hold a lepidolite in their pocket.

The knowledge of the crystals and their makeup is quite inspirational, especially when teaching or administering crystal healing with Reiki or other modalities that can assist people in their own self-healing processes. It is smart to take a course on crystal healing if you are intrigued, because there is a catch: some crystals aren't the best when they are next to each other within your personal energy space. If you have a random bunch of crystals and they are within three feet of you, they are within your aura, which means you can absorb their frequencies. This is great if you know what you need to balance, release, or advance. However, if you have several crystals that are simultaneously hyping you up and making you sleepy, this can seriously confuse your body's cycles and frequency! It's like taking a bunch of pills you may not need or vitamins that are way too high of a dosage!

Impacting your energy with items that raise and lower it at the same time is not a good combination, because it confuses things and muddies the intention. Certified crystal healers know their stuff regarding what synergizes and what does not for certain ailments, life goals, or fun journeys. I suggest that you either learn crystals or connect with the knowledgeable experts on crystal healing. Hello? I think we have already met. I am Jolie.

Let me tell you, healing with crystals and having a fun time with them to escape the daily grind is mind-blowing. Once you try harmonizing crystals and gemstones, you will be hooked. You will love how you can adjust, shift, release, balance, or advance yourself in your own home.

The Frequency of Crystals

Each crystal has its own unique frequency. This means that when you hold a crystal, its frequency can adapt to *your* frequency and release, adjust, balance, or accelerate your energy depending on the crystal's makeup.

There are also crystal points called generators. They are called generators because the geometric angles on the point cultivate more vibrational energy within the point's energy field, whether there are five or seven or more. In turn, you can feel the optimization of that energy in your energy fields. The crystal alone has a certain frequency to adjust, advance, release, or balance you, but the shape can amplify it. If you think that is super cool, you need to try meditating with sacred geometry sets. There are dozens of crystals that are selected and shaped into fantastic symbols.

When synchronized with purposeful, high-vibe meditations, crystals can be just what the doctor ordered! They can help you be more balanced, accelerate self-healing processes, create better mental thought processing, release old and negative frequencies, or create synergizing vibrations that enhance your mind, body, and soul.

I am going to teach you about beautiful crystals that have high vibrational frequencies. There are thirty-three powerful crystals to elevate your own frequency. They help bring a stronger connection to self or a specific purpose that you choose for your meditation.

Why Meditate with Crystals?

Right now, you can become a supersonic meditator using powerful crystals. Meditation with a crystal boosts the energy field, and holding a specific crystal for a certain purpose that matches your goal or intent will activate your senses. Remember, the crystal's frequency will adjust your frequency—but it is best to know what specific crystal can adjust or advance you correctly. If your purpose is to relax, you don't want to hold a crystal that gets you amped up and motivated. You wouldn't go to a heart surgeon if you broke your ankle, so use the *best* crystal to suit your frequency needs!

When meditating, we want our body to be relaxed, so you don't want anything cumbersome on you. One choice is to hold a single stone in each hand; another is to place stones beside you. All the crystals' energies will be synergizing with yours if they are within three feet of your body. Each meditation only uses two crystals. More crystals aren't always better for a meditative state of mind. It's not complicated; it's super easy.

In the next chapter, I categorize the crystals by meditation purpose. I also list all the crystals that are used in the meditations to help you get to know them and their uses. But first, let's discuss how to use your crystals.

How to Choose and Use Crystals

Of course, there are different sizes, textures, and energies emanating from the crystals you choose. Size does not matter. The feeling you receive from a crystal can be a sensation or an intuitive thought. These sensations can help you decide what to pick when you are shopping for crystals. You can purchase tumbled stones or rough, unpolished crystals.

Some people prefer a small tumbled stone because it is a smoother texture on the hand or body. Some prefer a rough, natural stone because they like the earthiness of its chunky appearance. There are many more choices. We have wands made of crystal specifically for meditation purposes. They are thin, rounded, and easy to hold. They are usually two to three inches long, and they come raw or smooth.

I know many of you have this question: Can I use or hold more than two crystals in a meditation? The answer is yes; however, you really want to be educated on which crystals harmonize together. There can be conflicting, confusing energy if you don't choose your crystals wisely For example, if you hold a crystal to connect to your angels, such as celestite, then hold another crystal that motivates you, such as pyrite, it may be harder for you to relax and feel the messages or vibes or your true intent.

Try using two crystals with one on each side of you. You will enjoy the ride and know that individual crystals are quite powerful. Meditating with crystals will change your life!

Cleaning Your Crystals

It is important to cleanse and charge your crystals before and after using them in a meditation, especially after a release session. You will want to cleanse your crystals after each use. We do this because your energy can slightly change the frequencies on a crystal, because it has an aura just like you do. The aura of a crystal can hold on to vibrations that are not original to them. When we work with crystals by holding or wearing them, their auras can pick up unwanted vibrations, because they can be barriers that protect your aura. It's like cleaning your hands after touching something dirty or contaminated; you don't want to hold it again until it is clean. There are lots of ways to cleanse your crystals. Here are a few options:

1. Sage
You can cleanse crystals by lighting sage. Some people love the aroma of sage and other cleansing herbs, such as mugwort. If you are not able to have smoke in your home, refrain from this type of cleansing.

2. Sun or Moon
Both sunlight and moonlight give off powerful frequencies that cleanse and charge crystals. You can lay the crystals outside in either light for at least four hours. This will be ample time to clear the unwanted vibrations from their aura and bring them back to their original frequencies. *Charging* simply means adding extra positive vibrations to their auras to amplify their original state.

3. Water

Water of any temperature cleanses well. Be sure to wash your crystals in clean water. Some people wash their crystals in the ocean. This is fine, but remember, if your crystals have a nice shine on them or are tumbled stones, their sheen could come off in salt water, which is an abrasive cleanser.

4. Sound

One of my favorite ways to cleanse crystals is using sound vibrations. I enjoy tuning forks, crystal singing bowls, or a Tibetan metal singing bowl. Occasionally I will clang my chiming bells or shake a simple handbell. All of these create frequencies that will cleanse your crystals and gemstones.

5. Other Crystals

You can clear negative vibrations using other crystals, too. The white mineral selenite is a self-cleansing formation that cleanses all other crystals if they are touching. It's pretty amazing. There are little bowls and long slabs of selenite that you can set your crystals on for cleansing. Himalayan salt is another way to cleanse your crystals; lay them on raw chunks or within salt particles.

6. Breath and Positive Intent

You can use your breath. Yes, I know this sounds nuts. Forced air with positive intentions works! Intentions have frequencies. This is mind energy I am talking about. You can say your intention of clearing your stones inside your mind telepathically while using your breath or outwardly using your voice, stating your intent aloud. You would do this by blowing on the crystals and simultaneously using your voice with a positive intention to clear all the vibes! "My crystals are clean and clear."

———

These are the many ways to cleanse those strange or icky vibes that have been absorbed by your pretty crystals! Now that you know how to stay clean, I invite you to meet the powerful crystals that will enhance your meditations to the maximum vibration.

Amethyst

Ametrine

Angelite

Apache Tears

Apophyllite

Auralite 23

Barite Rose

Bloodstone

Carnelian

Cavansite

Celestite

Charoite

Danburite

Fluorite

Hematite

Herkimer Diamond

Howlite

Jasper, *Bumblebee*

Jasper, *Ocean*

Jasper, *Red*

Labradorite

Moldavite

Moonstone

Pyrite

Quartz, *Clear*

Quartz, *Rose*

Quartz, *Rutile*

Quartz, *Smoky*

Quartz, *Spirit*

Selenite

Tiger's Eye

Tourmaline, *Green*

Unakite

Chapter 5
What Crystals to Use— Thirty-Three Powerful Crystals

In this chapter, I am giving you my favorite high-vibe crystals that work to create the purposeful frequencies you wish to line up with for your meditation. Know that you can shop your local stores for different crystals to meet your needs. I did pick ones that are bountiful, affordable, and most potent for the thirty-three meditations outlined in this book.

Take your time and read the crystal bios. You will connect with many right off the bat. For the ones you are unfamiliar with, get yourself into a store and feel their frequencies! It's nice to connect in person; if you click, you will want to work together quite often.

1. Amethyst

Amethyst is a beautiful purple crystal that relaxes you from head to toe. It is the most well-known crystal in the world. You can find it in personal collections, spas, hotel entrances, and anywhere one would want the space to feel homey and comfortable. It alleviates stress and releases tension in the physical body as it adjusts you for harmonious sleeping patterns.

Origin: Brazil and Uruguay. I have found that Uruguay has darker purple amethyst clusters than Brazil. Both countries have incredible, enormous mines!

Best Meditation Purpose: Amethyst is perfect for reading and healing the mind, body, and soul. It is great for protection and making a space feel comfortable and loving. It is perfect for relaxing the mind for those of you who overthink, and it opens the mind for visualizations and intuitive abilities. It vibrates high as it protects your energy fields and fortifies positivity.

Chakras: Third eye, heart, and crown.

Physically: It relaxes your body to the depths of your soul.

Emotionally: It makes you feel relaxed and safe.

Mentally: It opens the mind for insight and abilities that are extrasensory.

Spiritually: Enhances and opens you to divine energy.

2. Ametrine

Ametrine (spirit quartz) is in the quartz family. It is a combination of amethyst and citrine. This combination forms from iron and silica occurring in
the mineral. It was a crystal worn by Spanish queens in the seventeenth cen-
tury. This crystal is purple and golden yellow combined. It has a cactuslike
appearance. Spirit quartz brings a feeling of unity and vitality. Many believe
this stone opens you to connect with the divine. It can help you discover
inner wisdom and open innate knowledge.

Origin: Bolivia.

Best Meditation Purpose: Happiness, healing, and wealth.

Chakras: All chakras.

Physically: It aids with healing the nervous system and the related organs.

Emotionally: Brings peaceful feelings, especially when stress is in one's life.
It creates optimism.

Mentally: It creates clear thinking processes and helps with conscious, positive
actions.

Spiritually: It brings connection between the soul and the human—the
subconscious and conscious—for what you are doing in your life, creating
higher levels of contentment.

3. Angelite

Angelite (anhydrite) is a beautiful soft blue color, like a light blue sky on a perfect day. It is a telepathic connector and instills calmness of the psyche. This is a perfect frequency for connecting to those who have passed over into the light or for angelic communications.

Origin: Calcium sulfate mineral found in Peru, Britain, Egypt, Germany, and Poland.

Best Meditation Purpose: Connection with angels, guides, ascended masters, your source, gods, goddesses, Buddha, Jah, Jesus, Mother Earth, and Father Sky.

Chakras: Throat, third eye, and crown.

Physically: May help stimulate kidney functions, regulate water retention, and balance the excretion system.

Emotionally: Helps overcome insecurity and develop strong willpower.

Mentally: Helps with giving up obsessive behaviors and provides calming energy and overall mental strength.

Spiritually: Connection to universal energy and sources of the light.

4. Apache Tears

A semitransparent, black, mostly roundish formation. These have been used in some cultures as a token of condolences for those experiencing grief and loss. Apache tears bring soothing frequencies that can console and ground you to be present on Earth.

Origin: Mexico and Arizona. Volcanic ash that turned to glass, which is also called obsidian.

Best Meditation Purpose: Understanding the loss of loved ones and loss in general. Apache tears provide grounding and peaceful energy for those who carry them.

Chakras: Heart and root.

Physically: Grounds your body to feel more present on Earth.

Emotionally: Helps release emotional sadness and pain.

Mentally: Brings solace and understandings.

Spiritually: Creates a connection to those who have passed over and an innate connection to them through "signs" from the earthly plane to let you know they are visiting you.

5. *Apophyllite*

The unicorn crystal! If you place this on your third eye, it is quite possible to reach visualizations that open you to worlds beyond worlds! It is a hydrated potassium calcium sodium silicate. It is in the quartz family. It is a pyramid shape and a gorgeous, reflective crystal. It brings great power of truth about your past, present, and future. This is a perfect crystal for advancement meditation or past and parallel life experiences, including astral traveling.

Origin: Canada, Brazil, Mexico, and India.

Best Meditation Purpose: Connection to the past lives or divine energy of all the world's dimensions.

Chakras: Heart, third eye, and crown.

Physically: Helps with respiratory problems, nerve damage, and skin disorders.

Emotionally: Reduces anxieties and suppressed emotional issues.

Mentally: Helps release the focus on *stuff* in one's life. Brings balance and contentment.

Spiritually: Expands tranquil and honest powers. Apophyllite allows you to learn from past experiences.

6. Auralite 23

This crystal has superpowers—well, sort of. It has twenty-three minerals within its matrix, which makes it a super-high-vibration crystal. They are titanite, cacoxenite, lepidocrocite, ajoite, hematite, magnetite, pyrite, goethite, pyrolusite, gold, silver, platinum, nickel, copper, iron, limonite, sphalerite, covellite, chalcopyrite, gilalite, epidote, bornite, and rutile. It looks like a piece of dark purple amethyst, but it has touches of red. I love this piece of earth for its innate ability to cleanse, clear, balance, heal, and enhance me. If I hold one while I am meditating, it gives me the feeling of security and fearlessness! It opens my crown chakra while keeping me grounded; this enables me to receive accurate messages from my guides and angels. Once you work with this crystal, it will be number one in your collection for sure. I have a huge chunk the size of a bowling ball by my side when I am channeling messages for clients.

Origin: Canada.

Best Meditation Purpose: Keeps one simultaneously grounded and open at the crown. Restructuring, healing of the entire body, positive and safe feelings, and fearlessness.

Chakras: All chakras.

Physically: Said to reconstruct and heal the DNA; creates positive frequencies with all organs for beneficial functions.

Emotionally: Protection, grounding, feeling of support from Earth and light beings.

Mentally: Helps one process thoughts without overthinking; a direct line to the soul and one's higher self and sources.

Spiritually: Expands you to reach higher realms of divinity and universal power.

7. Barite Rose

Some call this the desert rose. It is made up of gypsum or barite and sand grains. It looks like an intricate design on a ball. You may say it has a rosebud likeness. Whenever I feel as if I need some balance, I hold one. Sometimes I get vertigo, and barite rose grounds me in my body. It is great for memory recall and equally good for balancing the physical body and clearing old issues from the present time. It helps me see lessons I may have not easily recognized otherwise.

Origin: Oklahoma, Kansas, and California.

Best Meditation Purpose: Grounding, strength, and memory clarification.

Chakras: All chakras.

Physically: Aids with throat and stomach issues and may clear nasal cavities.

Emotionally: Keeps one clear of old emotional baggage and helps one set healthy boundaries.

Mentally: Helps one express rather than depress; gives clarity of thoughts and actions.

Spiritually: Assists you to feel fully supported in life.

8. Bloodstone

Bloodstone is from the heliotrope mineral of the chalcedony family; it's a type of jasper. It is a solid green stone with small dots of deep red within it. This is a dark horse crystal. I rarely see people choose this stone, mainly because they think the name is weird. I get it. Bloodstone doesn't sound very appealing to me either, but its energy supersedes the name by miles! I meditate with bloodstone to improve my circulatory system. Sometimes I get stagnant vibes in my lower legs, so I hold one in my healing meditations. When I feel a bit out of control—this usually happens if I watch too much television news—I grab a bloodstone to release any negativity I picked up. I like to clear out negative frequencies before I go to bed, so I create my new positive frequency by doing a five-minute adjustment meditation with a bloodstone. I know I can sleep without those newscasters talking in my subconscious all night!

Origin: Australia, Brazil, China, California, Nevada, and Oregon.

Best Meditation Purpose: Cleansing, clearing lower vibes from the conscious and subconscious.

Chakras: All chakras.

Physically: Purifies, detoxifies, and improves circulation, lymph healing, balance, and immunity.

Emotionally: Allows you to release and let go easily; heals old emotional wounds and lets you feel you have control of your own life.

Mentally: Gives strength and confidence in all situations.

Spiritually: Makes you never feel alone, as you are connected to your source. Gives protection from all negative sources on Earth or beyond.

9. Carnelian

An orange stone that brightens your creative juices. This is a form of chalce dony containing hematite. Carnelian is packed with power for opening your bloodstream as well as your mindfulness. It helps one open to new abilities and mindsets that are consistent with manifesting one's desires. I enjoy an active meditation holding this stone, as it brings me more willpower to push myself toward positive physical action and great mental stability.

Origin: Brazil, Uruguay, India, and Madagascar.

Best Meditation Purpose: Creativity, activating sexual balance, and igniting inventiveness.

Chakras: Root, sacral, and heart.

Physically: Helps blood flow, circulation, and metabolism.

Emotionally: Stimulates and brings proper motivation in your life; helps you be receptive to new ways or ideas and opportunities.

Mentally: Brings creative thoughts to completion.

Spiritually: Confident connection.

10. Cavansite

I absolutely love this crystal. It is the brightest blue, similar to the color Archangel Michael is represented by. It is sometimes surrounded by brown sediment. This is one of my all-time favorites because it creates a frequency to reach your source and angel guides, including your higher self and all things on the purest dimensions. This great communicator stone brings clarity. It enhances all your senses, but especially clairvoyant abilities. Cavansite amplifies my clairaudient (clear hearing) skills to the maximum. I wear a ring with cavansite, and I feel a surge of ESP powers.

Origin: Silicate mineral from India.

Best Meditation Purpose: Communication, clear hearing, and clairvoyant abilities.

Chakras: Throat, third eye, and crown.

Physically: Kidney functions and ears.

Emotionally: Strong self-power.

Mentally: Instills positive verbalization and communication skills, including telepathy.

Spiritually: Hearing, feeling, and sensing connection to source and guides.

11. Celestite

Do you love angels and relaxing as much as possible? Celestite embodies both. It is a light blue, soothing crystal that bathes you in calmness. It awakens your mind to enlightened beings such as angels, cherubs, and ascended masters. It is perfect for a direct frequency to your loved ones who have passed over into the light realm, and it makes you feel appreciated and special. The crystal's energies can release old pent-up thoughts that need to be shifted in a soft, airy way. Celestite is made of strontium sulfite.

Origin: Madagascar.

Best Meditation Purpose: Communication with the light and all beings of positivity.

Chakras: Throat, third eye, and crown.

Physically: Helps heal bones, muscles, and organs and releases tension.

Emotionally: Helps release feelings of being boxed or trapped; brings conviction to change.

Mentally: Calms thoughts and gently helps one retain a peaceful mind.

Spiritually: Brings serenity from light beings and your source.

12. Charoite

This purple and black beauty is unparalleled for someone who overthinks! I know we all do this from time to time, but if you are replaying thoughts often, this is your gal. Charoite is a gorgeous specimen to say the least. It's hard to believe the bright or deep purple is natural, but it certainly is. Charoite can assist you with an identity crisis by letting you know who you really are. This crystal is blunt when letting you know that you are the boss of your life.

Origin: Siberia.

Best Meditation Purpose: To understand self, self-realization, and change.

Chakras: Sacral, solar plexus, heart, throat, third eye, and crown.

Physically: Relieves cramps, calms the nervous system, and heals heart issues.

Emotionally: Takes away stressors and calms your energy. Helps you be creative in your outlook on life.

Mentally: Overcomes resistance by allowing change to be understood and accepted.

Spiritually: Helps you stay strong in the current purpose of your life and helps you find a new path if needed.

13. Danburite

The stress releaser and body pleaser. Danburite is from the quartz family but has a distinct flat plank edge. Holding a danburite can change your life and outlook. This is the "no excuses" crystal. If you have addictive behaviors—whether from food, drugs, alcohol, or negative relationship patterns—danburite will set you straight and kick your butt until you are rearranged and balanced. Hold this powerhouse frequency to adjust your vibes for a better life.

Origin: Madagascar, Mexico, and Connecticut.

Best Meditation Purpose: To cleanse all negativity from your soul's imprint and energy on Earth.

Chakras: All chakras.

Physically: Helps reveal all underlying causes of heart, digestive, and addiction issues.

Emotionally: Brings selflessness and releases all constriction you may feel from life.

Mentally: Breaks down addictive thoughts that are taking over your mind, time, and behaviors.

Spiritually: Allows the notion that there is a beyond as well as karmic equality.

14. Fluorite

Fluorite comes in an assortment of colors: green, purple, white, light yellow, and rainbow. It is semitranslucent and is a must-have in your crystal kit. I call it the master healer stone. The frequency of this stone balances, adjusts, and regenerates. Meditation with this stone is especially healing on the physical, emotional, and mental levels. It is a gateway to the subconscious, and it cleanses and prepares one for newness. Fluorite gathers all negative frequencies and tosses them out like trash from your subconscious. It helps dissolve those blockages you created with your experiences; that's no fret for fluorite.

Origin: China, Russia, South Africa, France, Colorado, Mexico, Missouri, and Kentucky.

Best Meditation Purpose: Healing on all levels—physical, emotional, mental, and spiritual.

Chakras: All chakras.

Physically: Green fluorite helps heal bones and teeth along with posture, joints, arthritis, and respiratory issues. It is an overall ailment-healing crystal since it seems to assist in restructuring cells.

Emotionally: Purple fluorite helps release any blockages from issues current or past. Allows one to change the frequencies in the emotional layer of the aura to bring feelings of solace and a free spirit.

Mentally: Yellow fluorite helps release narrow-minded ideas and ideals. It stimulates centered and forward thinking.

Spiritually: White fluorite helps absorb higher knowledge and releases old frequencies and issues from parallel or past dimensions.

Please note that working with rainbow fluorite can add healing of all levels. Rainbow fluorite is quite pricey compared to one-color fluorites but is well worth it if you can find one.

15. Hematite

This silvery formation is influential in manifesting your desires. It can be magnetic, literally. You can purchase it as magnetic or nonmagnetic; I haven't found much of a difference in its abilities either way. Hematite is a slightly weighted stone and brings grounding and consciousness of one's actions. I love it because it makes me feel and notice all that is around me. I hold one to fortify my manifesting. I feel powerful frequencies connecting to the universe to bring goals and items and people I wish to attract closer to me.

Origin: An iron oxide in North America.

Best Meditation Purpose: Grounding and progression, self-forgiveness, and manifestation.

Chakras: Root.

Physically: Helps blood flow and the circulatory system.

Emotionally: Feeling of survival; an instinctual part of you has vitality, strength, and motivation.

Mentally: Makes you aware of desires you want to fulfill or bring to fruition.

Spiritually: Helps you develop stronger influences and connection for a beautiful life on Earth.

16. Herkimer Diamond

If you enjoy watching movies, this crystal is for you! Herkimer diamonds can make a person incredibly visual within meditation and sleep states. It is a crystal from the quartz family—clear and brilliant with double-terminated ends (that means it has a point on each end). This double termination releases and enhances your frequencies at the same time. Size does not matter with this crystal; all Herkimer diamonds pack a big punch of *wow*. I love using this crystal with moldavite to get out of this world. A Herkimer diamond is a great amplifier for any other crystal. It amplifies the vibes of other crystals to maximum power. If you want to find your soul's purpose, hold a green tourmaline and a Herkimer in each hand and let the information flow. Herkimer diamonds really are everyone's best friend for meditation.

Origin: Herkimer, New York.

Best Meditation Purpose: Provides amplification of frequencies.
Induces vivid journeys and insightful, detailed feelings.

Chakras: Throat, third eye, and crown.

Physically: Enhances vitality and strong visuals.

Emotionally: Powerful, loving feelings.

Mentally: Clarity of the mind for decision-making. Helps fortify your intentions, vivid dreaming, and astral travels.

Spiritually: A connector to divinity and realms other than Earth.

17. Howlite

Natural howlite is white with gray marbling. You can find it dyed blue, usually labeled and sold as blue howlite. It consists of calcium borosilicate hydroxide. I call it the focus stone. It is great for learning, helps enhance your memory, and assists anyone with ADHD or unsettling mind issues. It brings the best calming frequencies as it lets go of the sporadic vibes.

Origin: Canada, California, Turkey, Russia, and Mexico.

Best Meditation Purpose: Focus, steadiness, and calming of the mind and body.

Chakras: Solar plexus, heart, throat, third eye.

Physically: Assists in healing throat and ears.

Emotionally: Releases stress and anger. Best calming stone ever! Howlite helps with positive communication and verbal interactions.

Mentally: Assists with gaining focus and a positive direction of energy; unburdens the mind.

Spiritually: Connects one to the present.

18. Jasper, Bumblebee

The happy crystal! A bold yellow-and-black stone that awakens your vitality. I hold a bumblebee jasper to feel light and fun and happy! Looking at one is just as pleasing as it creates creative ideas that I can write down or proudly express. When I feel like I've lost my mojo or need some uplifting, I meditate with bumblebee jasper. I notice I really feel honored and grateful to hold such an interesting piece of earth in my hands.

Origin: Indonesia (near Bali).

Best Meditation Purpose: Pure bliss, happiness, success, and creative awakening; honor bestowed within as self-respect.

Chakras: Root, sacral, solar plexus, heart, throat.

Physically: Helps the immune system and strength.

Emotionally: Courage and expression.

Mentally: Stimulates honesty and self-worthiness.

Spiritually: Truth and honor with self.

19. Jasper, Ocean

Earthy and pure are the vibes you get from this beauty. You can find it in shades of pink and white with shells or pieces of inner earth embedded inside. I like to imagine where the crystal has been and where it tumbled over the years of its formation. It reminds me of the beach; I feel like I can breathe deeply in and out while holding one with ease. I connect closer to nature and earth and become quite creative visually. There was one time when I was wearing a necklace with ocean jasper and I was in a disagreement in my own mind about something, I remembered that my decision did not have to be so black-and-white, that I did have other options and remedies for my situation. It was nice to look outside my own box.

Origin: Madagascar.

Best Meditation Purpose: Strong imaginative and inventive visualizations.

Chakras: All chakras.

Physically: Heals skin, helps digestion, and dissipates tumors.

Emotionally: Helps stop patterns. Enables you to look beyond what is in front of you to see other options and avenues.

Mentally: Renewal, resolving any conflicts or discernments.

Spiritually: New beginnings, appreciation of Earth and the ocean.

20. Jasper, Red

Hercules? Well, maybe. Holding a red jasper grants power over and above the norm. At least that is how it makes me feel. I can say red jasper gives me confidence and strength and a great attitude! Best word to describe me with red jasper is *supersonic*.

Origin: California, Utah, Idaho, Wyoming, and Washington.

Best Meditation Purpose: Structure, grounding and strength, and good luck.

Chakras: Root, sacral, solar plexus.

Physically: Body fortifying, strength of muscles, and power of brain.

Emotionally: Confidence, manifesting powers.

Mentally: Stable thoughts, constructive views of self and others and life.

Spiritually: Protection and abundance of life.

21. Labradorite

This is one of the most gorgeous crystals you will lay your eyes upon. It holds blues and grays and bright hues of gold, green, and some shades of orange. It looks like a blue butterfly's wing. Magical and uplifting. It is made of feldspar. "The seer" is the nickname for labradorite. You can open up your third eye to ignite your psychic intuition, read auras, and feel gosh darn incredible while meditating with labradorite. I know many of you will remember this crystal because you will associate it with Labradors. This association is perfect as dogs are highly intuitive and use all their senses. Labradorite opens you up to universal knowing, paths that show you the light worlds, and beyond. Your skills of the magical metaphysical world will open and excite you with a labradorite crystal.

Origin: Canada and Madagascar.

Best Meditation Purpose: To open psychic abilities, clairvoyance, telepathic communication, protection, and karmic healing.

Chakras: Third eye and crown.

Physically: Amplifies healing.

Emotionally: Relieves past traumas; protection.

Mentally: Aids in prophetic visions and how to create with this knowing ability.

Spiritually: Helps inner healing of past karmic issues.

22. Moldavite

A meteorite that fell to Earth, moldavite is a glasslike substance whose origins NASA couldn't identify. Moldavite is a tektite mystery that landed in Czechia in 1786. Some say it was inserted in the Holy Grail and other precious artifacts. There is only one place in the world to find it, so make sure you are purchasing it from a known dealer or trusted source. Its name comes from its place of creation near the River Moldau in Czechia. It is chipped into many designs and sold by the gram. It is quite expensive as it has to be extracted over time. The good news is you only need a small piece to feel its power. Once you engage with its vibrations, you will be able to transform to a higher frequency. You will notice while meditating with a piece that you become more worldly and intuitive, recognizing the synchronicities around you and in the world we live in. It can be felt instantly at a touch: a rapid heartbeat or a sensation in the heart area to the crown of your head. Many have said a sensation of soothing shocks is felt over the entire body. I have worked as a crystal healer for many years, and Moldavite will transform a person to a higher evolution of themselves. I can only hold it when meditating because it takes me swiftly out of my body for a space journey. I love that feeling, but I cannot wear it as jewelry or I would not be an earthbound person! However, I have friends and clients who can't live without wearing it because it balances them to be more Zen. It cuts their stress and, for some people, lessens their A-type personality to become humanly tolerable! People love the feeling of the journeys it gives and the anxiety it relieves. It is perfect for someone using marijuana to switch to moldavite. Moldavite usage can save you lots of money and possibly your lungs!

Origin: Czechia.

Best Meditation Purpose: Out-of-body experiences, positive transformation of self.

Chakras: Solar plexus, heart, throat, third eye, and crown.

Physically: Helps with anemia, flu symptoms, ADHD, and Asperger's.

Emotionally: Transformation, freedom, release of all ruling energy.

Mentally: Brings full expansion of the mind.

Spiritually: Heightens dreams and prophetic visions. Takes one to a higher vibration for inner knowing and true respect of humanity and extraterrestrial existence.

23. Moonstone

Moonstone can certainly bring out your feminine energy. It is known for connecting you to the goddess that you are! *Self-discovery* is the best word to describe moonstone. While working with moonstone, you will notice your intuition rise as self-worth and your identity come to the forefront. Moonstone is of the feldspar family of minerals; it's a creamy, sometimes translucent stone with a white-blue sheen. It is perfect in jewelry because of its incredible beauty. There really is no other stone that compares to it. I have a few rings and a pendant of moonstone; they seem to really help me shine when I need a boost. I wear them mostly near a full moon, since occasionally the full moon's energy can kick me off-kilter, and a moonstone crystal keeps me more balanced. It is a crystal that works with cycles, such as cycles of birth and menstruation. If you are looking to conceive, this is one to hold or meditate with for preparing the body for motherhood. It also is known for cycles of completion. Many endings create new beginnings in your life. I have spoken to people about endings, specifically about love or friendships ending. This is a subject that comes up quite a bit in psychic readings. I notice people fear closure more than a new beginning. I believe we need to reprogram that fear because new beginnings are sensational! It is more than a second chance, it's a smarter, new, better you. We all need to remember to take note of the lessons learned after completion. This is a growth spurt—emotionally, mentally, and spiritually—for you! Change is good. New *is* exciting!

Origin: Sri Lanka, Madagascar, India, and Brazil.

Best Meditation Purpose: Help with cycles and completion of cycles, safe traveling, and mind journeys.

Chakras: Throat, third eye, and crown.

Physically: Menstruation, birth and ovaries, reproductive systems of all genders.

Emotionally: Brings inspiration and admiration to self and others to be able to proceed with tasks in life; helps with knowing one's identity.

Mentally: Helps realize the cycles of life and the body's rhythms.

Spiritually: Opens intuitive abilities and ESP and helps one connect with the divine feminine.

24. Pyrite

Some people call it fool's gold because it actually looks like nuggets of gold ore. They can joke all they want, but pyrite can bring abundance of money and manifested desires to your doorstep! Hold a pyrite while in a manifesting meditation and connect with frequencies that are matched and heard by the universe. Pyrite magnifies positive frequencies as well as empowerment of the holder. Need a jump start? Pyrite will activate and motivate you to start and complete any task.

Origin: Spain, Colorado, Montana, and Washington.

Best Meditation Purpose: Abundance, vital energy, truth, and loyalty.

Chakras: All chakras.

Physically: Stimulates liver, intestines, and detoxification of the body.

Emotionally: Powerful feelings of prioritizing what is important to you, motivation, confidence, and willpower.

Mentally: Wealth and abundance of mind, body, and soul. Instills equal energy with self and others.

Spiritually: Uplifted and strong manifestation connections to the universe and vibrations on Earth for positive abundance.

25. Quartz, Clear

The most famous crystal because it is a clear channel of strong frequencies. Quartz comes in many shapes, from points and pyramids to obelisks and pointed clusters. All are powerful for amplification of any other crystal to power up a room and generate a frequency within you that cleanses all negativities and clears your path for greatness. Crystal quartz is in our computers and radios! A quartz crystal is inserted to create high frequencies in radios for connection. I know. That is super cool. Obviously if it carries and transmits in technology, it is just as incredible for you to hold one or two in a meditation!

Origin: Arkansas and Brazil.

Best Meditation Purpose: Clarity and amplification of your frequency.

Chakras: All chakras.

Physically: Aligns your chakras and balances your meridians for positive cycles of the body and its organs.

Emotionally: Stabilizes feelings of uselessness, curbs greediness and selfishness, and lessens complaining and stress.

Mentally: Releases stress and ornery attitudes, brings enlightened thoughts of the world and self.

Spiritually: Brings a light of beautiful energy to your soul from the frequency that connects all with everything; oneness.

26. Quartz, Rose

Nothing is better than having trust in one's life. Love, compassion, and trust. Rose quartz is light to dark pink in color. You can find one raw, tumbled, or in just about any shape, including a heart. Meditation with a rose quartz brings hope and trust with a loving perception of life. If you need to mend a broken heart from a relationship or physically heal, meditation with a rose quartz is a priority. Rose quartz is especially helpful after a stressful day. I hold two in my hands and place both on my heart chakra, and I feel drenched with unconditional love. I recover and feel balanced and loved.

Origin: Madagascar, India, and South Dakota.

Best Meditation Purpose: Self-love and goddess connection.

Chakras: Heart, third eye, and crown.

Physically: Alleviates a stressed heart and lungs.

Emotionally: Brings love and compassion for self and others; trust and hope.

Mentally: Reduces stress, relationship issues, and past wounds of the heart.

Spiritually: Divine love, goddess energy, and all that is.

27. Quartz, Rutile

Rutile quartz is a milky or clear crystal—a silicon dioxide mineral with inclusions of rutile, which is a titanium oxide mineral. It may look like black lines within the clear quartz crystal. This crystal is powerful for those in need of reprogramming their life story's frequency. This means you can create a positive frequency and manifest what you want with your words and intent; holding the rutile quartz transmits that frequency to you. Rutile quartz is a tool I use with many clients to stop old patterns and addictive behaviors, such as drinking or binging, using drugs, and engaging in unbalanced relationships.

Origin: Brazil and Madagascar.

Best Meditation Purpose: Recovery from addictive personalities and the establishment of new patterns to replace old or negative vibrations from the auric fields.

Chakras: Solar plexus, heart, throat, third eye, crown.

Physically: Allows the body to receive healing.

Emotionally: Self-realization and feelings of love, comfort, betterment, and change.

Mentally: Prevents weak thoughts from becoming actions.

Spiritually: Helps promote solace and forgiveness for all aspects of self; brings healthy knowledge and foresight from your guides, angels, or divine source to become who and what you want to be.

28. Quartz, Smoky

Are you a bit spacey? If you are, smoky is for you. It can ground you to become productive and present. Smoky quartz has a slight or super dark gray color. It can alleviate negativity placed on you as a thought form or erase what you innocently "picked up" from everyday life. Smoky can make you feel wanted and accepted on Earth, with emotions of purposeful living. Smoky quartz can increase the probability of encountering synchronicities in your life and call in some energies that are watching over you to calm you.

Origin: Colorado, New Hampshire, Madagascar, Australia, Switzerland, and Scotland.

Best Meditation Purpose: Defending self from unwanted energy from others or the energetic environment. Protects and shields the aura.

Chakras: Root.

Physically: Relieves stress and pain from the body, especially the joints.

Emotionally: Helps you cope with and understand life's curveballs.

Mentally: Gives alertness and mindfulness of your surroundings so you can take action.

Spiritually: Releases unwanted junk from your energy fields.

29. Quartz, Spirit

This crystal (also known as cactus quartz) can be hard to find. It is amethyst and citrine that has grown together in a cactus shape. It appears as light purple with a golden hue from the citrine crystal. Spirit quartz held in a meditation ties your human self to your soul. The understanding of your conscious and subconscious on a soul level is fearless and peaceful. It can raise your level of enlightenment and guide you to express your life with great understanding and compassion.

Origin: South Africa (Magaliesberg Mountains).

Best Meditation Purpose: Gratitude and connection to source and all light beings, especially self-connection to the all-knowing higher vibration—you!

Chakras: Solar plexus and crown.

Physically: Calms and heals current ailments with frequencies of unconditional love.

Emotionally: Helps you achieve your dreams and goals and be less judgmental of others.

Mentally: Strong concentration and focus.

Spiritually: Sacred Earth energy and unconditional love vibrations; connects you to your higher self and soul.

30. Selenite

The cleanser crystal. Selenite is a hydrous calcium sulfite mineral; it is a form of gypsum. It is white and sometimes clear white in appearance. It can easily dissipate with water similarly to salt, so make sure you do not clear or cleanse it with water or any liquids.

Selenite is perfect for crystal grid work. If you place eight or more selenite sticks in a space in your home or office, it can create a vortexlike feeling and bring in angels, guides, or those of the light realm. If you work with selenite longer, you can visit a past or parallel life experience. Selenite is a cleansing stone because it erases frequency patterns in your auric fields from this lifetime and others. You can dismantle these patterns after you recognize they do not serve your highest good. You can additionally use selenite to clear out negative vibrations that are emitted from cell phones, computers, and anything that places harmful vibrations in your aura. It can keep your space or location clear of negative vibrations that may want to stick around, whether they be negative talk from others or low-frequency attitudes or dark entities. I suggest a short cleansing meditation while holding a selenite stone or stick to clear all your chakras and aura layers from any harmful frequencies at least once a week.

Origin: Oklahoma and Mexico.

Best Meditation Purpose: Cleansing and clearing, releasing negativity. It can also bring you to past or parallel lifetimes.

Chakras: All chakras.

Physically: A pain reliever and body relaxant.

Emotionally: Lightens your mood to be more carefree and fun.

Mentally: Allows you to let go of irritating people, places, or circumstances; shifts your ideals for betterment.

Spiritually: Purity and innovation of spirit within self; help with past or parallel life connections and realizations in current life. Strong transformation. Think of this mineral as a power washer. It can cleanse you as far back as another lifetime!

31. Tiger's Eye

This is one of my favorite protector stones. I have used this stone since I was eight years old, not knowing that it was a strong shield against negative energy. I think of it as the dark horse because it carried me through rough nights as I constantly experienced strange energy coming through my window between ages eight and fourteen. The color is a golden brown and it has brilliant markings. You can also find blue tiger's eye. The blue is deep and sometimes has yellow tinges within it. It is absolutely gorgeous. The golden tiger's eye is most common, as blue tiger's eye crystals are pretty rare and expensive. Both are incredible warriors that protect you physically and psychically. If you feel like you are getting attacked by negative or black energy, grab your tiger's eye! On the lighter side, it brightens your outlook and helps you be fearless. It can assist in healing your eyes and bringing strength to your overall body and psyche.

Origin: South Africa and Australia.

Best Meditation Purpose: Grounding, being present, and feeling content and protected.

Chakras: Root, sacral, solar plexus, crown.

Physically: Can help regulate adrenal glands; all eye-related healing; can keep you present in the moment.

Emotionally: Strength and protection with great understanding of self-power.

Mentally: Sharpens your thoughts and wits.

Spiritually: Brings protection and strong urges to connect to knowledge from above sources or earthbound frequencies in nature.

32. Tourmaline, Green

A green aluminum borosilicate with a hexagon shape, usually grown within white sediment. Green tourmaline in general is a pricier crystal. The bigger and better quality grades of tourmaline can range dramatically in price, but they are well worth it! Tourmaline is a healing crystal for the heart and spiritual part of any human and any part of nature. It creates a vibe that cradles you as it informs you of your greatness. I pair a green tourmaline with a Herkimer diamond and receive honest messages from my soul about how to go about my current life. Meditation to find purpose is important as we change over time and our purposes complete or shift. We all need to feel appreciated and content to fulfill our purpose, and this crystal will let you know how to create and aspire wholeheartedly.

Origin: Brazil, Pakistan, and Africa.

Best Meditation Purpose: Soul connection, finding your soul's purpose on Earth, connecting to self on all levels of existence. Becoming balanced and whole.

Chakras: Heart, throat, third eye, crown.

Physically: Helps induce healing of the entire body.

Emotionally: Brings love and unconditional self-love and connection from your source.

Mentally: Helps you understand how to allow flowing thoughts and accept change.

Spiritually: Lets you become whole, unified with self and the divine.

33. Unakite

This is the gazer stone; I also call it the "who am I, where am I" stone! First of all, it is a green stone with pink flecks in it—super cute. It works with your root chakra to keep you grounded and knowing who you are. If you are forgetful, it helps bring back some memory and know-how. I laugh about it, but if you seem to be in a fog or wearing "hazy goggles" in life, you need a unakite in your pocket and definitely need to meditate with one often. Unakite can transform negative emotions to positive ones and give clarity and self-realization.

Origin: North Carolina, Lake Superior, Michigan, Canada, Africa, Brazil, and China.

Best Meditation Purpose: Finding your identity or allowing re-creation of self-identity; grounding, memory enhancement.

Chakras: Root.

Physically: Reproductive system, skin, and hair; helps memory.

Emotionally: Balances moods. Serenity of self, deep look into desires and current tasks in life. Assists with coherence.

Mentally: Patience; helps one adhere to structure and timing.

Spiritually: Balances your positive and negative aspects to be harmonious in your connection with others on Earth and beyond; looking through all angles of life.

There you go! That was all the high-vibration crystals. They can be found in local crystal shops. Make sure you are purchasing authentic crystals from your trusted suppliers. Now we check out the crystals that are specific to your purpose. This next section has a list of crystals that fit best for certain meditations, such as connecting with self, intuition, insight, mind travel, and spirituality. I include protection and releasing crystals for those in need of some cleansing. Then I add the perfect crystals to help you with physical and emotional healing and mental processing. Of course there is a list for everyone's main concerns of love and abundance! I conclude with out-of-this-world planetary and moon-shifting crystals that can adjust your frequencies during extraordinary cosmic times in your life.

Chapter 6
Best Crystals for Meditations

Crystals will change your life. Meditating with crystals is incredibly powerful, enhancing your vibrations to raise your frequency and adjust it accordingly. I obviously love the vibes crystals offer, because these gorgeous earth chunks can be multipurpose.

If you didn't know, the planets and moon cycles affect our bodies and psyche. The shifting of the planets can shift us since they also hold and emit vibrational frequencies that affect the earth and all that is on it. It is nice to know you can use those cosmic opportunities and the shifting of them to your meditating advantage! In the following pages, I list a few advantageous cosmic occurrences and the crystals that work well for that specific purpose.

Meditation with Self

We all need a little time with ourselves! It's good to get in touch with what we need and what we need to release. These crystals can assist you to do well with both. I know sometimes we are in touch with our physical bodies but often take for granted our emotional and mental health; meditating with yourself can reform and connect those frequencies that may be currently severed from your mind, body, and soul. We need this connection to feel whole and balanced to have a happier, more fulfilled life.

- Amethyst
- Bloodstone
- Charoite
- Jasper, bumblebee
- Jasper, red
- Labradorite
- Quartz, clear
- Quartz, rose
- Unakite

Meditation to Connect to Psychic Abilities and Insight

If you are into evolving, this is how to do it—working with high-frequency crystals that open and enhance you to your highest, best self and your source. We can tap into unconditional love energy, which can be your god, angels, ascended masters, Mother Earth, Father Sky, Jah, or any other source. We all have these innate abilities, but some of us just haven't tapped into them yet. Everyone is intuitive. Some people feel too much pressure to become intuitive or be the best at it. Take away that pressure; it comes naturally. I teach a workshop called Psychic Skills. I teach people to use their senses and show them how to bring forth and trust "the knowing." I teach my students that we all are gifted—some of us are born with ESP, telepathic, and clairvoyant skills, while others just have to learn. They can tune in to their mind and senses as fabulous psychic adapters, then allow the energy to be revealed. I compare learning these super abilities to a pro athlete's abilities. All of us can hold a basketball and learn the game, but not all of us naturally do it easily, and not all of us are instantly pros. Pro athletes have practiced their game—plus they were born athletic. All in all, we all are intuitive, and some of us are innately intuitive, but that doesn't mean you can't learn the skills to be a pro! Did I mention that these crystals listed below help you become a pro? These tools rock!

- Amethyst
- Labradorite
- Moonstone
- Quartz, clear
- Quartz, spirit

Meditation with Nature and Mind Travels

These lovely energies will awaken your soul. They can take you up and out of this dimension and then bring you back to Earth. They can assist you in cleansing and healing issues from the past and the present. Looking for a temporary escape? Hold one of these crystals.

- Apophyllite
- Barite rose
- Jasper, ocean
- Jasper, red
- Moldavite
- Selenite
- Tiger's eye

Meditation with Loved Ones Passed Over

Trying to reach a loved one who has passed can be an emotional situation; however, it can be quite rewarding to feel their presence by using crystals that enhance your telepathic and clairvoyant abilities. Some people will experience a vision that pops into their mind or feel the presence of that loved one brightening their day. These crystals can raise your current frequency, which in turn elevates the unseen wire that brings you a sign of existence. You can receive that inner knowing that they are at peace.

- Apache tears
- Quartz, clear
- Quartz, rose
- Quartz, spirit
- Selenite

Meditation for Spiritual Connection with Archangels, Deities, and Beings of Light

These ascended masters are the highest beings of light closest to your source energy's frequency. This is the frequency of unconditional love. Holding one of these crystals during a spiritual connection meditation can unleash the vibrant love that calls these beings to your side for higher and innate knowledge. You may feel an enlightened buzz as you have them by your side or in your hands.

- Ametrine
- Angelite
- Auralite 23
- Cavansite
- Celestite
- Labradorite
- Moonstone
- Quartz, spirit

Physical Healing

Our physical bodies are affected by daily wear and tear; we need to give ourselves attention. Our physical energy body is just as important as our mental or emotional frequencies. It's important to adjust ourselves as needed and support ourselves—we can set the intent to let healing begin. These crystals can help repair and restore vitality and possibly DNA.

- Auralite 23
- Bloodstone
- Carnelian
- Fluorite
- Hematite
- Howlite
- Tiger's eye

Emotional Healing

This trio of crystals will pull out unwanted frequencies that may have been embedded for many years or lifetimes, then bring unconditional love to fill those voids and create wonderful, new, inspiring outlooks and positive, visual ideas and ideals.

- Danburite
- Jasper, bumblebee
- Quartz, rose

Mental Processing

Get out of the junked-up mind space. These crystals will clear your erratic vibrations by healing with stable light frequencies.

- Auralite 23
- Fluorite
- Hematite
- Howlite

Releasing

Got junk? Get relief. These crystal energies can balance and relieve you of unwanted stresses. Their powers lift layers of nonessentials from your aura and chakras. Identity crisis? Bring the *real you* out. Cleansed, strong, and ready for a purposeful life.

- Apache tears
- Auralite 23
- Danburite
- Moldavite
- Quartz, smoky
- Selenite

Love and Relationships

Want to bring in love from others or address issues with relationships? Need to fortify self-appreciation? Hold a rose quartz. This crystal strengthens self-love and compassion for others. We all need some self-care; rose quartz is the winner for this situation.

- Quartz, rose

Abundance

Money and greatness come from this dynamic crystal duo. The combination of citrine and pyrite ignites your desires and goals. You may also feel a zest for life holding these two motivator crystals.

- Citrine and pyrite together

Protection and Cleansing Self and Space

Auralite is always the all-in-one crystal because of its twenty-three minerals; it's a fix-it and heal-it crystal. Danburite can pull the yuck out of everything and anyone; this really is as strong as it gets. Danburite is not for the weak, because it can be intense as it helps you release. Smoky quartz gently releases and brings the barrier you need to protect self and space. Finally, nothing cleans up everything nicer than selenite! I call it the "white wonder wand." All these crystals are the best of the best!

- Auralite 23
- Danburite
- Quartz, smoky
- Selenite

Planets

Not familiar with how planets can affect our energy? Well, first of all, you must know that all the planets move around the sun and Earth in a certain rotation. When that rotation gets disrupted or changes, it can affect us. Why? Because each planet holds a specific frequency; this frequency can change Earth's frequency, especially if that particular planet moves closer to or farther away from Earth than normal. The planet can also go into a retrograde position, all of which affects Earth with a special frequency that can in turn disrupt our normal lives. Our frequency changes as well, and sometimes it doesn't change so nicely!

Now to explain the term *retrograde* to you. When any planet is in what astrologists call "retrograde," that means the planet is rotating backward. In the metaphysical world, when a planet is in retrograde, it can make our energy feel stuck. The retrograde planet spinning backward or standing still in turn makes us humans feel out of sorts, boxed in, and like we're thinking in circles. If you have a day when you really feel off but cannot identify any obvious issues, it is likely the planets or a planet has moved abnormally or is in retrograde.

Now, even though retrograde can bring some not-so-great outcomes for us on Earth, it can still be utilized for positive gains. You can come out with super advantages simply by knowing that a retrograde planet's meaning is usually the opposite of its regular meaning. A retrograded planet can recorrect what is needed in a person's life so they can relearn or relive an important experience. It is a perfect time to manifest and perform research if you know any planet is in retrograde.

As humans, our bodies work in cycles. Think about it: we have menstrual cycles, we are born, we live, we pass on. When a planet is closer to Earth, farther away, or in retrograde, all these positions can affect the earth's energy or the earth's aura. Humans have auras, and as the planets affect the earth's aura, they affect our auras. Think about the tides of the ocean as they are affected by the moon's cycles; we as humans can be affected as well.

Remember, each planet has its own frequency, and each planet represents something different to us on Earth. Here is a list of each planet's frequency and how it could affect us.[8]

Earth: 194.18 Hz—Grounding, wanting to be present on Earth.

Moon: 210.42 Hz—Cycles of life and body functions.

Sun: 126.22 Hz—Strength and happiness.

Pluto: 140.64 Hz—Revealing what is needed to be whole.

Mercury: 141.27 Hz—Good communications, arising lessons.

Mars: 144.72 Hz—Decisions and opportunities.

Neptune: 211.44 Hz—The ability to let go as needed, to flow.

Saturn: 147.85 Hz—Karma, positives and negatives of life.

Jupiter: 183.58 Hz—Luck and abundance, overall opportunities, strong changes in career.

Venus: 221.23 Hz—Relationships with partners, family, and friends.

Uranus: 207.36 Hz—Change and awakened energy.

During a new moon, our body is open to receiving self-healing a bit more than any other day. This is your cue for a self-healing or manifesting meditation. Within three days of a full moon is the best time to connect with deceased loved ones and spirits. The same goes for Mercury when it is in retrograde. Since Mercury is the planet of communication, retrograde is the best time to connect with other realms. It is not the best time to communicate any major dealings with other humans since we are off-balance in that aspect of our energy during that time. When Mercury is moving forward, communication among humans is easier. You can always connect with these light frequencies or loved ones passed over, but Mercury in retrograde is a great time to enhance that connection. Please note, if we are friendly, kind, and supportive of a positive frequency as we ask for angels, spirits, and guides to visit us on this earthly dimension, they usually oblige. We can also visit

8. Hans Cousto, "The Planetary and Chakra Frequencies," http://www.luminanti.com /SYNOPSIS%20Planetary%20and%20Chakra%20%20Frequencies.pdf.

them through our mind's frequencies and connect to them in their dimension; this is an astral travel or "visitation" to their world.

Here are the best crystals to use during cosmic times:

- Moonstone
- Cavansite
- Auralite 23
- Quartz, spirit
- Moldavite
- Angelite

———

It is great to have a go-to page for your meditation needs. Please use these crystal listings often; you can easily look up the crystals that will bring stronger vibes to your sessions. I suggest you try each of the crystals in all the sections. It is insightful when you notice which crystals may be stronger or feel better for you and your purpose. We all have our own unique frequencies. Have fun and experiment. Keep an open mind—expansion is priceless!

Part 3
Meditation Practices

Chapter 7
Meditations to Get Started

On the next pages, you will get into a great vibration mode and move forward with your meditation of choice. If you need to relax the mind and body to get you feeling open, you can use these meditations.

Now is the time to get your tools of choice, such as your crystals, aromatics, and comfortable space indoors or out. If you need extra boosting, give your crystal or Tibetan singing bowl a few plays or just use your voice and say *ohm*. These energies will raise your frequency to a higher level.

If you feel you need some assistance in your preconnection, I offer a few guided meditations on my website Crystaljunkie.com. There, you can download the polarity meditation, which was made specifically to sync your body and mind. After completing that guided meditation, you can continue with your own connection to your higher self.

Mini Meditations

Let's raise your frequency. Listed below are three mini meditations. Three short and easy ways to create a powerful, high frequency in just a few minutes. Remember to first note your current frequency (one being the lowest, ten being the most fabulous, highest, and happiest). After you finish your mini uplifting meditation, gauge yourself once again to see if you feel a higher vibe. If so, you are on the right track! This is your self-proof. You have raised your vibes!

The Generator

Holding a crystal and being receptive to their beautiful energies can enhance your meditation session. These crystals can be called generators. My suggestion for the mini meditation is holding a clear quartz crystal with a point on one end. You can also use an amethyst crystal, which helps open your mind's eye and relax your body. You can pick one of the tools from chapter 3 to get yourself vibing high or try one of these mini meditation techniques.

Breathing and Sensing

This is a breathing and sensing technique. Picture something beautiful in your mind. I like to visualize a rose. Now, try to see it up close. Imagine the smell of it. Imagine holding it. Notice each of the petals and count how many there might be.

Take a deep breath in, all the way, and then release that breath. Release it with a long push out, making a bit of noise with the breath. Do this a few times—I suggest three or more to relax you and release tension in the body. The vision just brings you to a happy mindset.

When using the rose as the happy object, we use the senses of vision, touch, and smell. Doing this opens all your gifts. I call them "gifts" because they enhance our experiences. Practicing these techniques can help you connect better to your higher self.

Raised Repeater

Another quick and easy meditation is something I call the "raised repeater." If you have a minute, you can raise your frequency by repeating a phrase. This is an active-awake mini meditation. You can be in your car, sitting, or just about anywhere, but keep in mind that you will be repeating a phrase out loud to get your energy going. I repeat this phrase six times. "I am smart, beautiful, and kind." Then I repeat this additional phrase another six times. "I am happy, healthy, and safe." I end with repeating the word *love* six times. Notice your energy and how you feel. I always feel like a ten after this meditation.

The Gift

This next mini meditation might sound silly, but it works to raise my vibes. This is "the gift." Wherever I am, I can do this (except while driving)! I visualize in my mind that I am receiving a gift. I see something instantly, such as a book or a stack of money—sometimes it is just a ball of white light, which is meaningful to me because I feel white light is my source gifting me beautiful life. Once you see your gift, imagine both your hands holding it. Really know you deserve this wonderful gift. As you are holding it, say, "Thank you; I happily accept this gift because I am worthy of this gift." Your energy shifts as you allow yourself to receive something "valuable." Remember, it has to be a gift valuable to you. This raises your frequency.

I continue to visualize the gifting about three times. The gifts can be the same or different. Three seem to be quite enough for me! If it takes more than three to raise your frequency, just go for it!

Journaling

If you like to journal, keep some paper and a pen near you during your meditation. I like to use a mini tape recorder to share my thoughts and feelings. Follow that if you are inclined. Please don't use your cell phone. Interrupting electromagnetics are best kept away from your peaceful space.

Journaling is a great indicator of progress. If you are working toward a specific goal or self-healing, writing down details of your session can be very revealing if you are on the correct track. I had a client who wrote in her journal each session. She was concentrating on abundance of money and appreciation for what she received. As she journaled her meditation sessions, she realized from her emotions and visions that she was blocked due to her early childhood trauma of a family member who would consistently undermine her confidence. If she hadn't written down her findings, she most likely would have just continued to try harder and harder to complete her goals. However, revealing this information made her meditate on her past and let go of resentments of that person that she held in her subconscious. Now knowing she can release that old energy emotion to become who she desires, her goals come easier and faster, and she feels deserving.

Autowriting

I have been asked many times if automatic writing is spiritual. I can quickly answer yes. Yes, autowriting is spiritually guided. It can be guided by your all-knowing you, which is your higher self or soul. It can be conducted by a spirit—someone you know who has passed over into the light or a different realm of existence. It can also be induced by ascended masters, angels, and other beings from other spaces on Earth and beyond. If this sounds attractive to you, let me share how to allow the autowriting to flow.

First, set yourself up like you're doing a meditation. Have your space clear and cleansed, safe and secure, then make sure you have a great flowing pen and a pad of paper. This is a combination of methods; it is a mindless and awake meditation. You will want to raise your vibrations to a ten on our scale, so playing a singing bowl or voicing your vowels can get you there. Proceed to set the intention: "I allow myself to be guided with this pen and paper, receiving visions, thoughts, words, and feelings that can channel through writing. I know they are from [your source]."

Please be polite when asking the source to be present with you on this Earth dimension. They will come if you are truly needing guidance or want to connect in a loving session. Please note that when you receive a connection, you may draw a picture, scribble, or write words. Allow the information that comes through to be natural and unedited—be mindless. It is not uncommon to feel as if an unseen person is placing their hand on yours and helping, guiding you as if they are holding the pen with you to write. When you stay on a higher frequency, the messages are clearer. If you become fearful, that lower frequency can bring unclear or skewed information or thoughts that may be from your own conscious or subconscious. I explain this because you want to be pure in the messages received, and the best way is to be fearless and mindless, allowing the energy you invite to help you write. If you expect too much, it makes it that much harder for you to automatically write. If you receive only a few messages or scribbles, that is a great start! It does take practice and trust to become a fluent autowriter.

Once you have relaxed and received, make sure you complete your session by closing, thanking your visitor and giving them gratitude for coming to you. Autowriting is like a phone call. You are picking up the phone, dialing someone's number, asking for them specifically, and talking to them. Once the conversation is over, you thank them and hang up for the call to be completed. It is really that simple. Sometimes you can just imagine the visitor to be there in front of you if you are visual; that can enhance the session. Another way is to imagine connecting to a white light, "calling in" to feel that connection energetically, and then telepathically talking to them. You must be on a consistently high frequency to keep the connection live. I stress that you maximize your frequency to be able to automatically write, as that enhances all your senses to be a good conduit of these messages.

The best crystals for autowriting are cavansite and auralite 23 or the combination of a clear quartz generator and spirit quartz. Experiment with both combinations and see which tunes you in best!

Ready, Set, Meditate

This is how it works. I organized the thirty-three meditation purposes into the five meditation methods. I listed two powerful crystals or tools for each meditation. I added intention and opening, easy guidance, and closing and gratitude directions. All meditations work best as a twenty- to sixty-minute session. Do what you feel comfortable with. Your body and mind will bring the awareness to your senses.

For those of you who worry that you will forget what to do, I suggest you record the directions. Simply record yourself saying the words verbatim from the meditation you choose. Then play it while you are in the relaxed mind state. If you don't feel your voice is best, ask a friend or a person you feel has a comforting voice to do it for you!

As you conclude your meditation, please make sure you take at least one minute to say the closing and gratitude that is provided in each meditation. This will bring completion to the meditation. This is important because if you were floating or somewhere in another state of mind, you need to come back to the present! You can also place both your feet on the ground. Tap them against the ground three times and say, "I am present. I am happy, healthy, and safe." This is just a positive intention that brings you back into the present moment. If you fall asleep during a meditation, that can be amazing, so just allow yourself to. When you awake, you can state the same grounding intent.

Remember, all the meditations are highly vibrational. You can do them anytime you need to balance, release, or advance. Choose one that calls to you today and go from there.

Chapter 8
Thirty-Three Meditations with Powerful Crystals

This is the best part of the book! Let's reset and raise your frequency to be the best it can be. You have thirty-three options of prime meditations. The five methods are labeled so you can find one that suits you for your daily meditation practice. I list the method, the purpose, the power-boosting crystals, the intention for opening, your easy guidance, and your closing with gratitude.

Nonactive–Slightly Awake Meditation

Nonactive–slightly awake meditation uses all your senses in a completely relaxed conscious and subconscious state. This meditation practice may include connecting to your higher self, adhering to the frequency of your soul, visiting with loved ones who have passed over into the light, enlightening self-realization, releasing negativity, meditating to nothingness, administering healing to your physical body, or enjoying a perfect full moon cycle.

1. Meditation with Self

Purpose: To connect with your true soul. This meditation will instill a frequency that connects all of your being to your imaginative mind. Your self-power induces confidence, and once you allow your conscious and subconscious to become one, your soul will be unified. This meditation will assist you in strengthening your ability to be powerful in loving ways, less abrasive, and less self-critical.

Best Crystals: Green tourmaline will bring connection to all of you that exists: conscious, subconscious, and the soul. It also delivers a string directly to your higher self, the all-knowing you. It can dilate your purpose. Quartz boosts all positive frequencies you hold and amplifies them to a higher level.

Intention and Opening: "I am connecting my soul, the purest part of me, to be in alignment with what my needs and wants are for my life. I allow connection to have inner knowing and understanding of my happiness and purposes as they change in my life. I can balance and know who I am gracefully and lovingly. I am one. I complete me by simply giving myself permission to hear and feel my inner voice. I am asking for my soul to speak to me through my senses."

Easy Guidance: Allow your inner voice to be heard by noticing any sensations in your body or any visuals you experience with your eyes closed and as your body is completely relaxed. Holding your chosen crystal in each hand, it is time to give kudos to yourself.

"I am grateful to be with all of me—my physical, emotional, mental, spiritual, and soul selves—my conscious and subconscious. Thank you for connecting and showing up. I love you."

Speak in your inner mind and say, "[Your name], I love you. You are always doing the best you can to help others and yourself. You are great at balancing your life and will continue to be. You are amazing, your energy is light to be around, and you fill a room brightly. You only speak with positive words and thoughts to match. Your actions are mindful as you handle all situations with respect and honor." Happily reply to yourself by saying, "I accept these compliments."

If there are any conversations about how you want changes in your life or improvements, this is the time when all of you is listening. Be detailed and truthful. You can be long with this meditation or super short and sweet. Calling all of you in is the strongest connection you can create. This breaks all barriers with all aspects of yourself.

Closing and Gratitude: "I would like to thank the all-knowing me, my soul, and all that exists of me. I know that sometimes I can be difficult, but I am glad we had this wonderful talk and connection. I love you, me, and all we are. Let us all be synchronized and love every life we have together."

2. Meditation with Loved Ones Passed Over

Purpose: To contact a person who is no longer on this earthly plane.

Best Crystals: Apache tears create frequencies of Earth reaching the beyond, providing love and peace from both worlds. Rose quartz communicates your loving intentions directly to your loved one.

Intention and Opening: "I am, and I allow myself to be, open to receive information and contact through my senses from my loved one. Please may I ask [state the full name of the loved one] to come visit me in my meditation. I would love to feel your presence from your energy vibrations and accept all visions, thoughts that pop into my head, and feelings as signs from you. Thank you."

Easy Guidance: While you are relaxed in a seated or lying position, have a paper and pen near you. Place the Apache tears and the rose quartz next to you. You can keep them in a pocket anywhere on your body or by your sides near the hip or heart area. Take three breaths in and out and focus on the person you called to visit.

You will start having visions, thoughts, or sensation in your body. You may also notice some shifts surrounding your environment. For example, this could be a bird or butterfly or sound out in nature that might let you know your visitor is present energetically. Write down or just feel and notice. This may be brief, so let it be and don't force "more." The slight things you notice are really the true contact!

Closing and Gratitude: You can personalize this to your loved one. Here is one I use often:

"I am grateful and thankful for you, and I hope we can stay connected. I appreciate any signs or messages as well as emotional feelings I know are particularly from you. I love you."

3. Meditation to Nothingness

Purpose: To feel weightless and have burdens disappear, so all you are is energy. Vibration that is flowing.

Best Crystals: Angelite opens your senses to higher-consciousness frequencies. Moldavite enlightens and brings an invitation for your soul to elevate.

Intention and Opening: "I am and I allow myself—I give all of me permission to bask in nothingness, as I am safe and protected as I do so. I can travel outside my body form with my mind. I am totally relaxed and happy to experience mind bliss."

Easy Guidance: Once you are in your comfy space, place the moldavite in your right hand and the angelite in your left. You can place them by your sides as well. Begin by noticing if your hands are relaxed, then your shoulders; wiggle them and loosen them up. Then take a breath in and out; take a few more breaths in and out.

Imagine your favorite color that is relaxing to you. With your eyes closed, visualize it on the wall above you. Imagine that color is warm and cozy and where you would like to be. Feel that color above you. Notice if you're feeling a wave of calming energy vibes from the moldavite crystal. You should notice a small sensation of movement in your body from your heart area to your head. This is allowing you to become one with the mind space.

Lie all the way back as if you are going to fall asleep. It's fine if you do, but until then your head and mind will only be floating, like that color above you, and you become weightless. Weightless like that color. Weightless like the sky. Infinite and continuous, it's free and flowing. You are just that. Lighter and lighter, up and up you go with that color, free and weightless, happy and just there. Allow yourself to just be there until you are not.

Closing and Gratitude: "I am grateful to have been in my mind bliss. I was relaxed and felt safe, and now I am back in the present moment, loving life."

4. Meditation with Archangels and Deities

Purpose: To connect with a specific archangel, deity, or being of the light. You can learn from their expertise and unconditional love frequencies.

Best Crystals: Angelite enhances intuition and all your senses as it is a crystal of strong communication with the light beings such as angels, gods, and goddesses. Celestite emanates similar frequencies that create the telepathic bond or portal to receive messages from using your senses.

Intention and Opening: "I am and allow myself to be balanced and open to receive only information that is for my highest and greater good and the good of all those involved. I am asking a guide named [add the specific angel or deity or ascended master here] to please come and guide me with insight and knowledge. I am grateful for your assistance."

Easy Guidance: As you lie down in your relaxed position, place your celestite on one side of you and your angelite on the other side. Begin by breathing in and out deeply and push out your breath; it's okay to make a bit of noise when you are breathing out.

You need to balance your chakras to receive information as a clear conduit. Imagine a white light washing over your body and cleansing you. It moves from the bottoms of your feet slowly over the tops of your toes and to the top of your feet. Take another breath in and breathe out louder.

As the white light cleanses and protects, it is aligning you. Try to feel the color white washing over both your ankles and up your shins. This is a healing, protecting white light. As the white light moves over your thighs to your left and right hips, notice if one hip feels lighter or heavier than the other. Take a few minutes to notice. If one hip feels heavier than the other, take a moment to place a strong green light of energy over that particular hip. Imagine this green light healing and lifting the heavy weight from it. Those heavy vibrations will go out of your body, out of your energy fields, and into the sky, where they can be recycled and renewed. You can take a breath in and out as you visualize the green light making your hip feel lighter. If both hips feel heavy, you can imagine this for one hip at a time. If both hips already feel light, move on with the white cleansing light.

Follow the soothing light to the base of your spine. At the base of the spine, the white light turns into a bright red. This is your root or base chakra; this is your grounding color. Focus on that area of your body for a minute or two.

Slowly work up to your sacral chakra, which turns the light into a beautiful orange, representing your creativity and your sexual organs. As you focus on that area of the body, feel strength. Take a breath in and out and focus on the area just below the belly button. This is your solar plexus chakra, your personal power and your emotions. Imagine this as a bright yellow, like the sun. Know that you are strong and powerful in loving ways.

When you are ready to move on, take a breath in and naturally out. Now it's time to move up to the heart chakra, the middle of your chest. Imagine the color green or pink here in this location. Allow it to be, and feel this unconditional love frequency on and around you.

When you feel ready to move on, bring the focus up to the throat chakra at the middle of your throat. Here, you will imagine a light blue energy calming and relaxing you. Let's stay here a few moments, and as you are visualizing the light blue over the throat chakra, we are going to move up to the third eye chakra, which is between your eyebrows. This area is emanating a deep indigo. It is opening all your senses to receive important visions or information from your higher self or your source energy.

Take another breath in and out. Your body is totally relaxed, and you are ready to connect your crown chakra, which is the energy from the top of your head all the way up, like an energetic white string of light. This string goes up to the sky and stars, directly to your source.

At this time, state one question you would love to ask your guide. State it clearly; this way, they can answer you better and more precisely. All you have to do is relax or allow yourself to fall deeply into your relaxation. Now we are going to have you connect to them with a white light. This is like a telephone line for them to know you are asking for advice and guidance.

Let's start by noticing the crown of your head. Say, "I would like to ask my source or those who guide me from the light to please give me a feeling, a vision, or a message that I can understand." Allow some time for anything that pops into your mind that may give you insight and feeling or emotions. If you aren't getting anything, that is fine; you may receive your messages within a day or so. Now it's time to forget about any focusing and just be in that mind space—that blissful relaxed energy—as you have high vibrations surrounding you. Just enjoy this feeling of euphoria.

When you feel ready, it's time to disconnect that white energy from your crown. Simply focus on the top of your head and notice it. This disconnects you. Now bring your focus to your third eye. Take a breath in and breathe out normally.

Your focus is now on your throat chakra. Take a moment here. Next, move downward to your heart chakra. Imagine that green or pink light there once again. The feeling is love, unconditional love. From that point, you will bring your attention to your solar plexus, the middle of your stomach, with the bright yellow.

Breathe in and out, moving down to the sacral chakra. The color orange represents your creativity and sexual energy. Breathe in and out, noticing and feeling with each chakra location. We are now at the base root chakra. This is bringing you back into the present moment; the color red represents strength, security, and stable energy on Earth.

Take another long breath in and a long breath out. You are fully balanced, cleansed and cleared, and perfectly aligned, healthy, and well. Take a few minutes to stretch your body, wiggle your fingers and toes, and open your eyes when you are ready.

Closing and Gratitude: "I would like to thank all the guides of light, and [say the name of the specific guide you called in], I appreciate you and am grateful for your messages and wonderful feelings of unconditional love for me. I hope to continue to receive helpful messages as we connect in future meditations."

5. Meditate to Your Soul's Frequency

Purpose: To connect to your soul's energy; to have your subconscious and conscious be bound in understanding what is best for you and your path on Earth. To be able to meditate to your soul's frequency to create good self-talks.

Best Crystals: Green tourmaline is precious, as it is directly linked to your soul's frequency with the help of the Herkimer diamond. Together they are superior earth elements.

Herkimer diamonds increase clarity, visualizations, and clairaudient abilities, optimizing the green tourmaline and your vibes.

Intention and Opening: "I am and allow all of me—my physical, emotional, mental, and spiritual energy and all that I am on Earth and beyond—to be synergized. This way, I can be at my full potential, do my best, and be loving and kind. I allow myself to be compassionate, caring, and kind while being strong and balanced."

Easy Guidance: Place one crystal on each side of your body. Lie down and close your eyes gently as you imagine a gold or white beam of light shining on your heart chakra in the middle of your chest area. Just imagine feeling that color as powerful and loving. Once you sense and notice that emotion from the light shining on your chest, allow it to move from the chest like a white or gold arch to your third eye area.

Imagine that same shining light beaming there. As the arch becomes thicker, you get a stronger sense of your soul and physical body connecting, feeling amazing and loved. The arch then creates another light beam from the third eye to the crown chakra. It can feel as if you are connecting to your god or source energy. Relax as you find all this connection making you slightly sleepy, release the thoughts of holding those light beams, and just allow yourself to sense or feel whatever comes at those moments, and if you feel like napping, allow yourself to do so. You created the connection, and it will stay whether you are awake or not, because all of you is synchronizing, as well as the crystals by your sides.

Closing and Gratitude: "I am proud of myself for taking the time to connect with all parts of my existence, allowing my soul to be connected to the earthly me. I am thankful that I brought forth the unity of me."

6. Meditation for Self-Realization Frequency

Purpose: To understand and receive insight for self.

Best Crystals: The clear quartz increases clarity and releases self-judgment or untruthful thoughts about yourself. Smoky quartz unleashes the woes and fears while vanishing all bad frequencies you may have adapted or created for self.

Intention and Opening: "I am and I allow myself to understand my mind and body. I would like to ask my higher self, the all-knowing me, my soul, to help me receive clarity and truly understand. Help me collect knowledge of my human self [state here what you want information, clarity, or knowledge of].

Easy Guidance: Take one long breath in and one long exhale out. Repeat this three times. Please breathe in and out at your own pace. Sit in a place where you feel comfortable and peaceful, indoors or outdoors.

Try to feel with your heart. Focus by holding your chest area with both hands. Then know your body and mind are now connected. Continue while focusing on asking equally for knowledge and self-realization. You can state this aloud or within. If you need to stop and get a paper and pen to write or add more details, please do this. Create your manifesting accordingly.

Say or write, "With this information, I will have self-realization of what I need to know in this lifetime to advance myself in all aspects of my life this year of [insert year]." Be specific. For example, doing better at school; letting go of negative relationships, prejudices, or selfishness; or being a victim of others taking advantage of you.

Continue with, "With this knowledge, I will be a better person. I will have self-love, and I can treat others better when I understand myself. I can teach others about my experiences and how they might relate to them. I want to have self-understanding as well as understanding of others; I will look through other people's eyes or situations.

"I will also understand myself. I want to know more about my body and mind. I want and deserve to live happier. My knowledge is freedom; I can have it and share it with others. I receive this knowledge and self-realization on [add date here] on the earth dimension."

You may have something that happened to you in your lifetime that you want clarity about; this would be something you would ask about specifically.

Closing and Gratitude: "I am thankful for my newfound knowledge and perspectives. I will work with them to keep me moving in a positive direction in my life."

7. Meditation for Release of Self-Negativity

Purpose: The purging of vibrations that are lower and repeated, such as resentments, self-hurting thoughts and fears, lack of confidence, and self-sabotage stemming from words or thoughts one holds over oneself.

Best Crystals: Danburite is a steadfast train that rolls through any weather, your bullcrap, facades you created, and any self-blame. Its frequencies break it all down so it can be swept out of your body and out of your energy fields for good. Rutile quartz keeps your frequency from going back to that same old track of negative doo-doo.

Intention and Opening: "I understand that I have allowed self-sabotage; I am now allowing and giving permission to change and adapt powerful loving thoughts, as everyone deserves good things and occurrences in their life. I am part of everyone. I deserve a positive, good life and good opportunities that allow me to move forward. I now accept these gifts and will take action when I am offered these gifts from other people, myself, and the universe."

Easy Guidance: "I release all fears or facades I created in my mind about me and my life. All that is negative, I am allowing myself to change. That includes changing my record, shifting my ideals, and becoming more honorable, trustworthy, and loyal to myself and others. I am a human being who has faults and can easily move them out—the emotions of them and my mental process of how I think about them. This way I can become all I truly want to be."

Closing and Gratitude: "I am always able to release any issues that arise. I am powerful in loving ways. I can create my own destiny; only I can release what I need to. I certainly am thankful that I understand how to dispose of any toxic energy with beauty and grace."

8. Meditation for Healing the Physical Body Frequency

Purpose: Setting frequencies for the physical body, mind, and soul to connect and allow self-healing.

Best Crystals: Fluorite and auralite 23 together are a powerhouse for adjusting and creating healing frequencies in your aura. Fluorite brings healing on all levels: physical, emotional, mental, and spiritual. Auralite 23 is the mack daddy in one crystal. It can protect, heal, restructure DNA, and create positive thoughts and perception.

Intention and Opening: "I am and I allow myself to activate my body to self-heal. [If there are certain parts of the body or organs you want to heal, name those areas of your body for this intention and opening.] This body part will be able to heal at a rate that my body needs. My mind and soul both know that we can adjust what is needed to be perfectly healthy, perfectly functioning in my human body on Earth."

Easy Guidance: Opening your mind to new possibilities is more than saying words, it is putting action to that thought. Many of us go to work, come home, and worry about all the things we need to do or have to get done. Take two minutes to breathe in and out slowly, then ask yourself, *Am I happy? Am I healthy? How does my body really feel?* If you can answer these in two minutes, you are more balanced than most. However, *feeling* answers is more important than simply stating the words.

Take the next eight minutes to notice how your body feels. Just focus on each body part one by one slowly. *Slowly* is the key word. Your eyes can be closed now and during this whole meditation if you choose.

First, notice your right eye and then your left eye. Notice how your lips feel, then the right and left ears. How about your neck? Bring your focus to each body part as you go along. Notice your right upper arm, then the left upper arm, moving down to each wrist, hand, and finger. Then trail back up into your chest. Slowly move to each and every body part one by one. *Notice* how relaxed you feel by the time you get to your last little toe. This is *noticeable action.*

Let's continue to the meditation. If you have a crystal or Tibetan singing bowl, play it for three minutes before visualizing and noticing. Place the crystals by the sides of your body. If you do not have a bowl to play, activate the energy by speaking the word *ohm.* Repeat the sound *ohm* eleven times. Make sure to breathe in and out between each *ohm.*

Continue by placing the crystals in your hands. With your dominant hand holding the crystals, write an imaginary number eight in the air. Eight is a magical healing number of infinite energy. This symbol brings infinite energy of what you intend, so you are bringing the infinity of wellness and positive health. If there is a specific organ or body part that ails you, air-write the eight-infinity symbol over that part of your body. You can do this as many times as you wish.

Let yourself just relax and breathe. Notice the shift in your mind and body. After a few more moments, focus on your third eye in the middle of your forehead. Imagine that same smaller infinity symbol is floating over your forehead, instilling the symbol of healing in your soul. Connect and know that healing is needed and that you can be repaired. Visualize this—no need to air-write it. Just visualize it in the colors of the rainbow or pick one color that resonates with you at that time.

Closing and Gratitude: "I am grateful for my body and how it synchronizes to become powerful and well. I know that I can allow healing in my body and all its intricate systems."

9. Full Moon Cycle Meditation

Purpose: Completing a cycle or closure of an event, a relationship, or a personal emotion and enhancing your overall energy frequency during the full moon.

Best Crystals: Herkimer diamonds enhance and advance your well-being and tune up your frequencies. The full moon's energy also amps up your vibes by cleansing and clearing your aura. Combine those with moonstone—a favorable crystal for positive travels, cycles of life, and purposes in our lives—and we can continue to manifest and reset.

Intention and Opening: "I am grateful for the cosmic energy, such as the moon and stars. They favorably guide me in my quest to complete and have closure. I am ready to advance and bathe in the moonlight's frequencies to charge my energy as it cleanses and clears me."

Easy Guidance: This meditation is best done outdoors, weather permitting. Basking in the full moon is definitely beneficial to your frequency! Place a Herkimer and a moonstone so there is a stone in each hand. Sit or lie in a comfortable position, and if you can, face up so you can actually see the moon over you. Don't worry if it is cloudy; the vibes still penetrate through to you. Now close your eyes and breathe in the outdoor air.

Closing and Gratitude: "I am blessed that I can enjoy Earth and beyond as a connection of all that is. I can synchronize my mind and my body to create what I want and need in my current life. I am gifted to be able to sense the moon's energy to fulfill and move me forward to my next quest."

Active-Awake Meditation

Active-awake meditations are when one is cognizant. You can inspire and bring goals to fruition with new moon cycles, bring important information from your higher self to be observed and retained, give thanks to those in your life and gratitude for all that exists, and notice conscious and subconscious instructions to heal yourself of drama, trauma, and anxiety. One of the most popular meditations people like is the meditation to correct karma or early life issues. All of these can simplify your life and raise your frequency.

10. New Moon Cycle Meditation

Purpose: Start a new cycle for goals and bring achievement. For this meditation, I love to use my labyrinth, walking within and back out of it. If you
don't have or can't create one, imagine walking into and out of one as I
describe in the Easy Guidance section.

Best Crystals: Moonstone is a cycle starter and a completer. It brings the
access you need in your chakras for change. The human chakras are vortex energy spheres similar to the symbol of the labyrinth and the cycle
of the moon. All boost and energize us and keep us on track to a goal of
completion. Pyrite is the force that sparks your energy to keep the eye on
the prize and is your best cheerleader to continuously keep you moving
until fruition occurs.

Intention and Opening: "On this new moon, I am awakening myself to be
open to new opportunities and blessings. I can complete any goal I set my
mind to, and I can also see it fully completed with success."

Easy Guidance: Set yourself at the beginning and opening point of the labyrinth while holding the crystals in your pockets or hands. Look at or imagine the spiral of rocks that create the labyrinth. Notice that all are placed
ever so imperfectly but intently into that spiral symbol.

It is a new moon cycle, so you can conjure your new goal by taking this
short, influential walk. At this moment, set your specific intent of what
your goal is. Take a few breaths as you word this in your mind. Then state
it aloud or again within yourself.

As you take each step forward, visualize or create a scenario where you
are working on this goal. Take steps one, two, three, four, and five, then
take a breath in and out. Fortify those intentions, visuals, and thoughts
with your breath going in and out. That is you accepting and confirming
your goal will be accomplished. Continue walking forward with positive
visualizations and scenarios until you reach the center of the labyrinth.

Once inside, look at the pile of rocks or the marking at the center
point. Breathe in and out, confirming your goals and desires have been
heard by the universe and heard by your soul. Place both crystals on exist-

ing rocks in the middle area of the labyrinth. This is your gift to the universe for hearing you, an energy exchange of goodness. At this time, you can once more visualize your goal coming to fruition. When you are ready to move your way out of the labyrinth spiral, with each step, state aloud or in your mind what will help this goal become reality. It can be gratitude, others who will guide or help you, or just your inventiveness, but each step recognizes the comradery of this goal becoming complete. Imagine what that looks like after a month and after a year when this cycle is complete as you step out of the labyrinth.

Closing and Gratitude: As you step away from the scared symbol and area, state that you are grateful to share your wants, needs, and goals with the universe, which will guide and aid you with their completion.

11. Meditation with Your Higher, All-Knowing Self

Purpose: To receive important information to help you in your current life; positive guidance for the present.

Best Crystals: Cavansite is my all-time favorite and a Hall of Famer in the rock world! Cavansite opens your ears, along with the rest of your senses, to become brilliant. It surpasses any misunderstanding because your clairvoyant abilities become remarkable. Then add clear quartz, the magical crystal that can do it all—from aligning your chakras to cleansing them—which brings on the heat of super clarity and abilities to decipher any messages you receive.

Intention and Opening: "I give myself permission to tap into my all-knowing self—the part of me that is only for my best interests and all those involved with my best interests. I am asking to become a clear, accurate channel of this source of me that will allow me to use my senses to receive information. This way I can autowrite all feelings, messages, signs, symbols, and all that connects me to positive information about what I am asking."

Easy Guidance: Place a notepad and a pen near you. Please use an easy writing pen, such as a light marker with no chemical smell. It is good to have a smooth writing pen because you will scribble a bit or write messages or draw anything you sense. Remember, if you don't expect too much, you won't be disappointed. Just allow and breathe.

Place your crystals next to your body with one on each side (cavansite on your right side and quartz on your left). Get yourself comfortable by sitting or lying down; faceup is best. Allow your hands to be weightless as they are placed on your solar plexus chakra, the middle of your stomach, and state your intention and opening. Visualize yourself performing a wondrous task that you perceive as powerful. It can also be superhuman.

Imagine introducing that powerful you to another part of you that may not be as powerful. Imagine shaking hands, hugging, or laughing together. Whatever you visualize as the other you, speak to each other in your mind. Each is giving compliments to the other. Allow yourself to feel the emotions of the conversations. If one brings negativity, imagine placing that word, feeling, or visualization in a wastebasket. When you feel the conversations, actions, or feelings have subsided, say, "We are one, and together we are complete. Let's always be our best."

Closing and Gratitude: Write visuals or feelings on a piece of paper. It's interesting and insightful to notice what you may have learned about yourself. Once you are finished jotting down your notes, thank all of you for contributing to any knowledge or insightful information to guide you in your betterment. Please make sure you ground yourself by tapping your feet on the ground and saying, "I am back in my body, happy and present on Earth."

12. Meditation for Gratitude

Purpose: Giving thanks for all you have in your life: people, places, and things. To become aware of the present moments that are precious, as each day is truly a gift.

Best Crystals: Barite rose is an earthy mineral that connects you to what you currently are accepting as an earthly being. Bumblebee jasper provides the happiness and pleasing frequency that embody our contentment with what we have and appreciate.

Intention and Opening: "I would like to ask the guides of light to come help heal me on a physical, mental, emotional, spiritual, and soul level; to keep me safe and protected here, now and beyond; and to bring me light and happiness. I am grateful."

Easy Guidance: This is a walking meditation. You can be on a treadmill, walking outdoors, or walking in a mall—wherever you feel comfortable. It is best if you know where you are going on this meditation walk, as you will be having some inner dialogue and will want to be on autopilot.

Take three long, deep breaths and three long exhales. Now place your crystals in your pockets. As you walk, you will notice different happy or neutral sights. At each stop, notice something that makes you smile. Keep noticing things that give you happiness. If you find something that does not make you smile, bring your focus back to what brought you happiness.

Do this until you stop thinking, because once you get to a happy mindset, you will stay on that frequency. If you get offtrack, bring yourself back to anything happy. If you are thinking about your responsibilities, that is the opposite of what we want, so stay in happy thoughts, like smelling something that makes you excited. When you are back where you started the walk, stretch your body, legs, and arms, and breathe in and out.

Closing and Gratitude: "I am able to appreciate my life and all that is in it: people, nature, my opportunities, my work, and especially myself. I am thankful for me."

13. Meditation for Emotional Healing from Anxiety, Drama, and Trauma

Purpose: Emotional healing from drama and trauma.

Best Crystals: Ametrine bestows loving, calm energy with a touch of happiness. Ametrine also helps one peek through the window of falsehoods to open the door to hope and harmony. Danburite is the enforcer of keeping lower frequencies out of your energy space, body, and mind, facilitating stable emotions and severing unhealthy habits, emotions, and relationships that no longer serve you. Danburite strongly enables mental and emotional healing frequencies as it wipes out the debris.

Intention and Opening: "I am and I allow myself to heal from other people's issues and my own issues and any misfortunes that affect or have affected me in a negative way. I can let go of these hurtful emotions and fears. I am strong, and I am tapping into my higher power to enhance my awareness and strength. I'm revising my life and dealing with what I need to with healthy, positive, amicable actions."

Easy Guidance: Once in your relaxing space, you can call in and kindly ask your higher power or a guide, such as Archangel Raphael, to assist you in your self-healing meditation session. Hold danburite in one hand and ametrine in the other. You may notice that the danburite feels stronger in one hand than the other. Switch them to feel any difference. Whatever hand you feel the strongest, leave danburite in that one. If you feel no difference, just continue.

Collect any negative thoughts or visions that give or gave you anxiety. Imagine placing them in a recycling container. Every thought or emotion allows you to feel and push those frequencies into that large imaginary pail. If you need to release by crying or yelling, give that a go. You are in your sacred or Zen space, so this is perfect timing.

Focus once again on the crystals in your hands and imagine a place where you will send those negative worries and all that is in the pail to be recycled. It is now nonexistent to you and can never return. Now repeat the intention: "I am and I allow myself to heal from other people's issues and my own issues and any misfortunes that affect or have affected me in a negative way. I can let go of these hurtful emotions and fears. I am strong, and I am tapping into my higher power to enhance my awareness and strength to revise my life and deal with what I need to in healthy, positive, amicable ways. I can do this. I am strong."

Take a few moments to feel the difference of the danburite crystal in your hand. Notice if it is lighter or heavier. Most likely the danburite will be hot or warm in your hand. Its frequency adjusted yours, and now it's time for you to take both crystals and leave them in the sun for four hours or more to cleanse appropriately.

Closing and Gratitude: "I am grateful to myself to be able to recognize my faults and turn those lessons into my powerful knowledge. I can let go of whatever and whoever no longer serve me. I know my self-power and can use it anytime I need to."

14. Meditation for Balancing Unequal Energy, Past Life or Early Life Issues, and Karmic Correction

Purpose: Balance unequal energy and correct past life or early life issues; karmic correction.

Best Crystals: Labradorite lets you see past everything to connect to your inner truth and intuitive abilities—past, present, and future—as needed. Pair with the harmonizing apophyllite that equalizes all emotional, mental, and spiritual issues from the past, morphing them into understanding from all perspectives, bringing forth forgiveness, and fortifying one's inner strength to let go and move ahead with knowledge that surpasses any book education.

Intention and Opening: "I give myself permission to release and completely let go of all emotions, all angst, and all fears from my past. I have learned about those experiences and how they may have been hurtful, but they gave me strength for today and every day moving forward. I can understand all actions that were involved through different perspectives, making me worldly. I know what's right or wrong in my current life. I am strong and can keep equal energy with myself, knowing that I have let go of negative vibrations that have kept me stuck. *Forward* is my motto, and my frequency is bliss."

Easy Guidance: With crystals in hand, blow on them as you use your power to cleanse and clear them. Your breath and the frequency of the crystals are open, and you are ready to release and revitalize. Sit back and repeat this: "I realize that having unequal energy with myself or others keeps me off-balance. It is not a burden to hold this energy, but I need to accept the lessons from it and move forward so no ties are attracted or created from negative feelings."

Now get yourself super comfy, close your eyes, and only visualize a way into a happy future scenario where you are successful in all aspects of your life that are important to you. Once you have had your visual experience, hold both hands open and place the crystals on your chest. Take three breaths in and out as a confirmation that you will be significantly happy with balanced energy. All karmic energy is now equal.

Closing and Gratitude: "I released all burdens from my past, present, and future. All karmic energy is now equal. I gave myself permission to create positive emotions. I have transferred my frequency, my imprint, to become clear and blemish-free. I am confident, full of love, and have filled my voids with the understanding that these were just lessons to create my newfound happiness."

Active Physical Body Movement Meditation

You can use activity and physical movement to become more grounded and present on Earth. This can be a daily reprieve, a meditation to retrain and reprogram your thoughts while moving your body—it can't get healthier than that! Meditation and physical activity are a perfect combination. We all need to keep ourselves in check and be the best we can with balancing meditation practices.

15. Meditation to Become More Present on Earth

Purpose: Connecting to be happy with your presence on Earth by feeling that you are needed and appreciated. Being present and grounded is appreciating the moments you are alive.

Best Crystals: Red jasper brings courage, determination, and sensible self-power. Blend these frequencies with tiger's eye's undeniable protection and bold strength that are aligned with earthbound elementals. They will convert your frequency to make you more present.

Intention and Opening: "I want to be one with myself and be present to enjoy life on a day-to-day basis. I will find something each day that gives me a purpose (small or large) to be useful and appreciated by myself, Earth, and others. I am mindful of what I do and say and know that I matter."

Easy Guidance: This practice is really fun. You can pick any place since you will be walking around as you do it. Mindfully notice any object or person. It can be anything, from a leaf on a tree to a local supermarket. As something catches your eye, I want you, if allowed (with a person, please don't touch them!), to look at and say in your inner voice something you like about that object.

You are only allowed to talk nice! You can't go into how you would change it or hate the color. This is about positive inner talk and noticing; be mindful of your surroundings. It is projecting positive thoughts from you to other people or objects. When you do this, your energy frequency will shift to be higher and bring you to the present moment, as you are fully aware of your surroundings. Be aware that only you control your thoughts. This meditation is active and strengthens you to be a worry-free person.

Here is an example. If you are looking at a dress in a shop, find one thing you like about it. It can be the color or the design. You don't have to love it, but notice it for what it is and reveal one good quality. This is practice for when everyone becomes telepathic in the years to come. I am kidding. Or am I?

Closing and Gratitude: "Today has been a good day. I noticed and liked several people, places, or things today, including myself for being a happy, purposeful person on Earth. Talking nice about everything brings me to a great vibration."

16. Retrain and Reprogram Your Thoughts

Purpose: Retraining and reprogramming your frequency meditation for self-betterment.

Best Crystals: Selenite cleanses all the old and strips your aura layers to be sensationally clean. The best part is that selenite only takes the bad vibes, so you continue to keep the positive template you adapted. Jasper brings in new ways to visualize what you want. It helps when you need to reprogram yourself with wholeness and worthiness with a perfect balance of adventure, lighthearted energy, and stimulation to create and adhere to what works best for your life.

Intention and Opening: "I can reprogram the way I think and make coordinating actions with my thoughts for betterment. I allow myself to change and teach myself this easy way to shift my mind through using visuals."

Easy Guidance: You can be doing something active if you are good at visualizing at the same time. If not, then stick to sitting while doing this reprogramming meditation. We start by using your imagination.

First, I want you to think of a meal. This meal is placed on a white ceramic plate. Keep visualizing as I describe it to you. It has one piece of broccoli and one sweet potato that is open and filled with cinnamon and butter. Imagine smelling these foods. They look ready to eat, and you can feel the heat and see some steam coming from the potato.

Now let that vision go. We are changing it up. There is a yellow plate. On the plate is a veggie burger. It has a bun that looks yellowish—very soft and fresh. The veggie burger is a green color and has a large piece of lettuce with ketchup, mustard, and a bit of mayonnaise on top of it. The top bun looks like it was squished on top of the lettuce and condiments. There is a side of curly potato fries—a healthy heap, but they are extra crispy, almost burnt. Maybe you can imagine smelling them and tasting them. Take a moment to notice. If you are able to see everything in detail, that is great!

Now here is one more. Imagine a round thin-crust pizza. It is a fifteen-inch pizza. It is still in the cardboard box. The top of the box is flipped up so you can see the whole pie. It has red sauce covered in thick mozzarella cheese that has melted over the entire pie. It has toppings of mushrooms and peppers. Small mushrooms from a can, and a green pepper sliced diagonally. You are smelling it.

Did you connect with the details of how the meals changed? You are so good at this you can create your own meal with all the specifics.

See, changing your mind to create a different scenario is easy. If you were successful in visualizing these meal scenarios, you proved you can reprogram yourself to anything you want. That is how strong your mind is. These types of meditations prove that you can do what you need to do—if you truly want to change. I was told early in my life that *sorry* means you will not do that again. Tell yourself you won't, and you won't. It's that simple; don't make it complicated with excuses and scenarios that keep you stuck.

Closing and Gratitude: "I am creative and can change my thoughts. It is effortless for me to take actions to reach my goals."

Meditation with Mindful Thoughts

Mindfulness is something we need to share with others. You can meditate and bring balance to all your energy centers and clear your mind of unwanted thoughts for true, clear thinking. You can learn to adapt frequencies to focus and/or adjust ADD/ADHD behaviors to become more structured. As you clear, you can know what you truly want: to love yourself, the ability to have positive relations with others, a good match for love, to move forward to manifest your desires, such as money, career, and a life shift. Instill excellent communication skills as you become an expert at balancing your mind and body, allowing simplicity in your life.

17. Meditation to Balance Body and Mind Chakras for Clarity

Purpose: Clear the energy and balance the physical, emotional, mental, and spiritual body. If you feel off-balance in general, this will get you aligned, grounded, and back on track with your emotions and mental processes. Sync up your spiritual connection to be strong.

Best Crystals: Auralite 23 is a chakra cleanse on its own! It has potent energy to whip your energy body into shape! Clear quartz's mighty vibes conduct your frequency like a finely tuned orchestra. All in harmony and grace.

Intention and Opening: "My intention is to become balanced, clean, and clear of all negativities that may have surrounded my energy fields and my physical body. I will be clean, clear, and balanced."

Easy Guidance: As you lie down in your relaxed position, breathe in and out deeply and push out your breath. It's okay to make a bit of noise when you are breathing out. This helps release any unwanted energy.

Bring your focus to the bottoms of your feet. Imagine a white light; this white light is going to wash over your body and cleanse you. From the bottoms of your feet, the white light moves slowly over the tops of your toes and to the tops of your feet. Take another breath in and a louder breath out. As the white light cleanses and protects, it is aligning you. Try to feel the white color wash over both your ankles and up your shins. This is a healing, protective white light.

As the light moves over your thighs to your hips, notice if one hip feels lighter or heavier than the other. Take a few minutes to notice. If one hip feels heavier than the other, take a moment to place a strong green energy of light over that particular hip. Imagine this green light healing and lifting the heavy weight from it. Those heavy vibrations will go out of your body, out of your energy fields, and into the sky where they can be recycled and renewed. You can take a breath in and out as you visualize the green light making your hip feel lighter. If both your hips feel heavy, you can imagine doing this one hip at a time. If both hips already feel light, focus on the hips with white, cleansing light. Once you are back to white light energy at both hips, follow the soothing light as it moves to the base of your spine.

At the base of the spine, the white light turns into a bright red. This is your root or base chakra, and this is your grounding color. Focus on that area of your body for a minute or two.

Then slowly work up to your sacral chakra. The color red turns into a beautiful orange, representing your creativity and your sexual organs. As you focus on that area of the body, you feel strength. Take a breath in and out and refocus on the area just below the belly button. This is your solar plexus chakra, your personal power and your emotions. Imagine a bright yellow like the sun. Know that you are strong and powerful in loving ways. Notice and feel the color yellow at the center of your stomach. Imagine that yellow like a round ball of light; allow it to become the size of a base-ball, then the size of a basketball. As it grows, you become more powerful and more loving. Stay with this strong feeling and color.

When you are ready to move on, take a breath in and naturally out. Now it's time to move up to the heart chakra, the middle of your chest.

Imagine the color green or pink here in this location. Allow it to grow, first bigger than your body, and then bigger than the room. Expand it while seeing the color in your mind's eye. Feel this unconditional love frequency on and around you. When you feel ready to move on, we are bringing the focus up to the throat chakra at the middle of your neck.

Here, you will imagine a light blue energy. It is soothing and calming; it allows you to be heard by others and speak kindly to yourself and the people in your life. Let's stay here a few moments. As you are visualizing the light blue over the throat chakra, in your inner voice, say some encouraging, helpful words to yourself: "I am great, I can speak kindly to others, and people love to hear what I have to say, because I am honest and truthful."

Once you have inner talk about only positive things, we are going to move up to the third eye, which is between your eyebrows. This area is emanating the color indigo. It is opening all your senses to receive important visions or information from your higher self or your source energy. Imagine feeling a deep indigo light at that area of your forehead. Take another breath in and out. Your body is totally relaxed, and you are ready to connect your crown chakra, which is the energy from the top of your head all the way up, like an energetic white string of light. This string goes up to the sky and the stars, directly to your source. All you have to do is relax or allow yourself to fall asleep.

Notice the crown of your head. If there are any messages you would like to receive, ask to receive them. Say, "I would like to ask my source or guides or those who guide me from the light to please give me a feeling, a vision, or a message that I can understand."

Allow some time for anything that pops into your mind that may give you insights, feelings, or emotions. If you aren't getting anything, that is fine. You may receive your messages within a day or so. Now it's time to disconnect that white light from the crown of your head. To do this, simply focus on the top of your head. Now bring your focus to your third eye. Take a breath in and out normally.

Your focus now moves to your throat chakra for a moment. Next, move downward to your heart chakra. Imagine that green or pink light there once again. The emotion is love, unconditional love. From that point, you will bring your attention to your solar plexus, the middle of your stomach with the bright yellow.

Breathe in and out. Go to the next location of the body, the sacral chakra. The color orange is for your creativity and sexual energy. Breathe in and out, noticing and feeling with each chakra location. We are now at the root chakra, bringing you back into the present moment. The color red is what you can visualize in this area of your body; feel the strength and security and stable energy of Earth. Take another long breath in and a long breath out. You are fully balanced, cleansed, and cleared and perfectly aligned, healthy, and well. Take a few minutes to stretch your body, wiggle your fingers and toes, and open your eyes when you are ready.

Closing and Gratitude: "I am back in my physical body, clean, clear, and balanced. I give gratitude to myself and all energy of light that helped me."

18. Meditation for Self-Love

Purpose: To feel complete in self-love, accepting yourself physically and accepting all that you are.

Best Crystals: Charoite is a boost of compassion that regulates your frequency to stay at a cherished high; it lets you know you continually deserve love! Rose quartz is unconditional in the admiration department of self.

Intention and Opening: "I am and allow myself to love my body and my mind wholly and totally. I love myself unconditionally."

Easy Guidance: Once you are in your safe place, place your rose quartz crystal in your left hand and the charoite in your right hand. Get comfortable by sitting or lying back, placing both hands and crystals on your chest, which is your heart chakra. Notice your breathing in and out at a normal speed, and bring your awareness to your heartbeat. Listen to its rhythm. As you become more in tune with yourself, try to visualize a pink heart that starts beating the same frequency as yours currently is; it is imaginary but feels real.

After two to three minutes, let yourself visualize loving thoughts and attributes of yourself. For example, "I am humorous, I am loyal, I am a hard worker, I am trustworthy, I have great eyes…" Notice all that is positive about you. Each thought or feeling is energy vibrations. You are absorbing all those positive vibes through your thoughts and words into your beating heart.

Closing and Gratitude: "I am proud that I can really trust and understand that I love and honor myself fully. I deserve good things and experiences, including attracting honorable, like-minded people in my life."

19. Meditation for Manifesting a Loving Relationship

Purpose: Manifesting a "good match." Since this is the most popular type of meditation, many of you may want to know the difference between the terms *soul mate* and *good match*. The term *soul mate* is used by many people. The spirit guides find it funny because they say, "We are all souls that live together." I believe this to be true. I loved this statement so much that I use it as the tagline on all my books and media. In this way, all humans are soul "mates."

A "good match" is a person who is equal to you in a loving relationship. A match who will best suit you in this life. You are to them as they are to you. You both love each other equally. Archangel Michael states that a human's good match is a person who has the same understandings and actions of love, honor, respect, and trust. That is what makes the core of a positive relationship.

Finding your "good match" entails a strong, loving relationship with equal energy exchange and similar values. This is described as the "core" of what you want and allow as your normal. (When I say the word *normal*, it means *what you believe is normal*. Not what I or anyone else thinks of as normal.) Happiness comes from *your energy*. When you glow with positive energy, others are and will be attracted to you. No one likes to be around negativity; it's draining. Everyone likes to be around positive and inspiring energy.

The angels want you to manifest this relationship. Make sure you add details of what you would want from your good match. Say this manifesting only once a week; otherwise, you are just repeating words, and the manifesting doesn't have the same intent and feeling to make it strong and heard. Concentrate. If this *is* important to you, you will make time to do it correctly!

Best Crystals: Rose quartz brings unconditional love of self and others. This is an equal energy exchange. Carnelian enhances attraction frequencies. I joke that it is like potent pheromones!

Intention and Opening: "I am and I allow myself to meet a [say your specific preference for your good match; you don't need a name] who has healthy habits, who is respectful to me, and I to them. They are attracted to me sexually, intellectually, physically, and emotionally, and I to them. We love each other 100 percent; we are monogamous to each other [if that's what you want]. We communicate properly and nicely to each other, and we understand each other's feelings and ways of thinking. We accept each other's normal; we are happy together, and we trust each other. We are each other's good match, and we deserve each other. We meet [insert a month and year] in the earthly dimension."

Easy Guidance: Take three long breaths in and three long exhales out. Do this at your own pace. Sit in a place you feel comfortable and peaceful, indoors or outdoors. Try to *feel* in your heart. Focus by holding your hands lightly over your chest area. You can do this with both your hands. Your body and mind are now connected.

Continue with your focus on "asking equally" to manifest your good match. You can state this aloud or within. If you need to stop to write or add more details, please do this. Make your manifestation accordingly. Please use the intention and opening outline.

Here are some options to insert if you choose. You may also add what *you* desire of your "good match."

- They have a good job.
- They are humorous.
- They are a happy person and love life.
- They are physically, emotionally, mentally, and spiritually available to you, and vice versa.

You both are attracted to each other and sexually compatible physically, emotionally, mentally, and spiritually.

- They have values similar to yours or values you admire.
- They have healthy habits and are of sound mind.
- You have a compatible "normal."
- You have the same four core understandings and actions of love, honor, respect, and trust.
- They are good looking to you.
- You are both available to meet each other (not attached to someone else via marriage or a binding relationship).
- They are abundant in money (if that is important to you).
- They are human. (I'm just being funny. I hope this is a given—laughing out loud.)

According to the angels, "You can't be someone's good match if they're not yours. This is equal energy exchange."

I believe that we can change our path in life by manifesting our desires and wants. However, based on my experience as a psychic reader, most people have difficulty taking action on new changes to shift themselves. This is solely because they have fears. This is why I love to share knowledge about how our mind and body frequencies can be shifted for the better. There are some people who believe everything is written before we are born. They feel we aren't able to change that. I ask them, "How are we able to manifest, then?" I have manifested along with thousands of others, and we are successful in manifesting our desires while using the energy exchange concept. Oh, just something to think about.

One strong revelation I had is that all humans are programmed by our experiences in life, our environments, and what we hold as our beliefs. This is something we can decide to change if we choose to. However, I also believe we have all been doing this living, learning, and experiencing forever, and all we know is eternity. I feel we are definitely moving forward with our lessons, but we are also just flowing around the parallels of all infinite existence. And a big group of us keeps playing our same frequencies! Do me a favor: manifest, and know you deserve what you are asking for. Use the energy exchange concept and see what you shift!

Closing and Gratitude: "Thank you, universe, for hearing my request in the form of a frequency. This way, my good match and I can connect and find each other easily in the time frame I am asking for. I am ready to receive, as we deserve each other."

20. Meditation for Manifesting Money, Wealth, and Abundance

Purpose: To create a frequency that attracts money and brings creative energy to achieve wealth.

Best Crystals: Pyrite and Herkimer diamond. Pyrite is a standout stone that attracts wealth and self-power, confidence, and knowledge that you are worthy. Herkimer diamond amplifies your energy; if your frequency is high, it will bring it higher. If you are adding another crystal, in this case pyrite, Herkimer will amplify the power of its energy. A Herkimer diamond is also the holder of true clarity and a direct connection to your higher power.

Intention and Opening: "I am and I allow myself to [work for, receive, find, and/or win] large amounts of money or [desired amount] or more. With this money, I will take care of my responsibilities, but I will live within my means. I will share and help others if needed."

Easy Guidance: Take three long breaths in and three long exhales out. Do this at your own pace. Sit in a place you feel comfortable and peaceful, indoors or outdoors. Try to *feel* in your heart. Focus by holding your chest with your hands. Then consciously know your body and mind are connected. You can state this aloud or within: "Money comes my way easily. I can earn it, I can win it, I can be gifted it, and I happily accept it, because I deserve it." This is a mantra you can say weekly when you need to boost your frequency, specifically to accumulate money.

Continue by asking equally for manifesting money and abundance. Trust that money will come your way. Know that you truly deserve this gain. You can state this aloud or within. If you need to stop to write or add more details, please do this.

Make sure you're manifesting accordingly by stating the amount you want and leaving it open to receive more. If you do this manifesting meditation monthly, note that you can change your details since you may need to tweak or advance as opportunity arises. If you decide to write it out, please write in detail what you want to receive, as your equal energy exchange for receiving your manifestation of money or abundance arrives through opportunities.

Please use this outline for your mental process of abundance. You can say or write your manifestation: "I can and I will bring money and abundance of opportunities to myself. I deserve this money to better my life and my family's life. What energy I give out, I will receive without expecting. What is deserved will come my way [desired date here] in this earthly dimension." It is important to genuinely mean what you are thinking and verbalizing, as your manifestation frequency goes out to the universe. Remember, you are also connecting with your intent consciously and subconsciously. All these frequencies make it powerful.

Here are other options and phrases you can add for manifesting money and abundance:

- What I strive for and my work efforts will bring money my way.
- Money can be a new job or a salary. It can be a raise or an upper-level position at a current job or a new one. It could be winning an item and selling it for money.
- I am open to receive money or values via positive ways.

- I will treat others, and all abundance I am responsible for, as I like to be treated—in a positive way.

Closing and Gratitude: "I am powerful enough to create vibrations that will bring opportunities of abundance and money. I will be aware and know I deserve this amount of money I am manifesting with equal energy exchanges."

21. Meditation for Job Changes, Career, or Life Shifts

Purpose: Manifesting a career, job, or life-shifting frequency change.

Best Crystals: Citrine and hematite. Citrine brings happiness, abundance, and positivity for all outlooks on life. It can inspire one to be their best. Hematite stimulates original thinking and successful dialogue of how to achieve goals. It can stop the self-sabotaging thoughts that bind a person from their successes. Hematite brings you to the present moment to act on the now and take charge to reach your level of contentment.

Intention and Opening for a Career Change: "I am and I allow myself to get hired at [job you desire]. I will receive a fair contract. Both of us will be happy with the contract. I will honestly do the best job I can. I will be the best employee I can be for [company/employer]. In return, the company pays me fairly. We are both happy and satisfied with the work I contribute. I receive this job [month and year], Earth dimension. We both help each other and respect each other in all aspects of business and work ethics. We have an equal energy exchange."

Intention and Opening for a Life Shift: "I am and I allow myself to shift my life. I want to allow change and become perfectly fine with change that is healthy and good for me and all those involved. I allow myself to see and feel strength and visions of what my better life can be."

Easy Guidance: Take three long breaths in and three exhales out. Do this at your own pace. Sit in a place you feel comfortable and peaceful, indoors or outdoors. Try to *feel* in your heart. Focus by holding your chest area with both your hands. Your body and mind are now connected. You can state this aloud or within. Continue asking for your new opportunity or life path.

If you need to stop to write or add more details, please do this. Make your manifestation accordingly.

Here are other options for asking for a job. They can be very specific if needed:

- Write in a company's name you wish to work for or a boss's name to hire you.
- If you have a specific field you are looking for, note that occupation.
- If you want a job in another location, list that information in the appropriate area.

When writing of changes, you want to manifest them in your life. You can list them as specifically as you need to. If you are not sure what the changes may be as of yet, you can just ask for positive, healthy changes in your life and say what month and year you'd like to adopt those changes. I feel you get the idea of this one!

Closing and Gratitude: "Thank you, universe, for allowing my manifesting vibration regarding my specific shift to go out and be heard and for bringing me a connection to realize what I've asked for."

22. Meditation to Improve Communication

Purpose: To speak to other people with mental clarity.

Best Crystals: Angelite allows you to speak smoothly and kindly with ease and can bring an angelic helper to guide you. Cavansite makes conversations amicable, kind, and noteworthy. It brings insight, knowledge, and impeccable communication skills, whether telepathic or verbal. An add-on tool you can use is a crystal or Tibetan sound bowl. You will also be using your voice for this one.

Intention and Opening: "My intention is to speak fluidly and mindfully. I am and allow myself to become my best at this skillset."

Easy Guidance: For this meditation, you will sit comfortably either on the ground or in a chair. If you have a singing bowl, keep it near you. Place both crystals in the bowl. If you do not have a crystal or Tibetan bowl, you can still do this meditation and it will be magnificent. In that case, place the stones by each hip. Now, let's warm up your voice as you will be stating mantras of the chakras. This will raise your vibration, and playing the bowl will amp it up a bit more. Hit your dowel against the bowl and say *ohm*. We are using the vowel sounds to activate your chakras and align them.

You can constantly play the bowl as you repeat each vowel sound. Take time to breathe in and out as needed, but say each vowel as if you are making it longer and slower. This way you can feel those vibrations throughout your entire body. As you voice the vowels, you can locate where in your body you may be feeling more energy flowing. This is such a fun and quick way to meditate. This can become a daily practice for those who are working on balance and communication skills.

- We start with the base root chakra and voicing UH.
- Then, follow with the sacral chakra below the naval area, voicing the vowel OOO.
- To the solar plexus with OH.
- The heart chakra with AH.
- Throat with the sound EYE.
- The third eye with AYE.
- And to the crown chakra and the sound EEE.

Once you are at the crown chakra, stay there a bit and repeat the vowel at least three times. When you are ready, start backward from the crown down to the root chakra. This will help ground you once you have completed your voice-activating meditation.

Closing and Gratitude: "I am powerful and assertive in my words and polite and honorable with my dialogue with others. I can ask for assistance, I can get my point heard, and I can converse with love and concern as needed. I will also be heard by others in positive powerful ways. I respect others and they respect me."

Don't be surprised if you get a lot of extra attention the day you do this meditation. Your vibes will continue to resonate from your aura and create such good energy; people are usually attracted to it—which is to say, to you!

23. Meditation for Focus, Mental Stability, and Calm

Purpose: This is great for people who need better focus and amazing for those who battle with ADD or ADHD.

Best Crystals: Howlite and ametrine. The combination of howlite and ametrine brings your frequency depth and control. Howlite creates stability and position. Ametrine allows the mind to feel relaxed as it heals any unbalances. Both together calm your energy and allow competent changes and steadiness.

Intention and Opening: "I am and I allow myself to be mindful of my tasks and actions. I allow myself to think about my actions in a manner that brings me clarity, soothing energy, and methods that help my life be easier than it is currently. I am calm and can take my time with what I need to feel comfort in my daily actions."

Easy Guidance: This meditation is nice and calming. Take both crystals, one in each hand. Place both hands on your stomach. Let them gently be there. If you want to move your hands away in a few minutes, that is fine, but leave the crystals on the stomach area or close to it. If your mind starts drifting to other things, bring both hands back to the stomach.

Imagine a light blue light at your stomach. This light blue is calming and will become the light that eases your feelings no matter what they are. This blue light is absorbing all thoughts. If you find a thought seeping into you, imagine placing it in the stomach area where the blue light and crystals lie. They absorb everything and recycle the thoughts into beautiful blue light. The more you place thoughts there, the stronger you become. Stay in this by making the blue light brighter and brighter. This is calming, and it brings your focus to be stable in calming yourself and your mind.

When you feel you are ready, take both hands from wherever they may be and pick up both crystals. Place them into the sunlight or in your cleansing selenite or singing bowl.

Closing and Gratitude: "I am empowered by knowing I have the energy to create my actions that give me structure. I can control my thoughts as I practice with meditations that are strengthening my mind."

24. Meditation for Balance of Mind and Body

Purpose: To bring the balance of body and mind for clarity.

Best Crystals: Clear quartz generator (or with a point) and ametrine. Clear quartz is a power source; it brings in vibrations that amplify and balance your body. It opens your third eye to create new outlooks that can be beneficial to those who stay stuck in a black-and-white mindset. Ametrine enlightens the mind, heals old thoughts, and brings the body to a relaxed state of being.

Intention and Opening: "I am and I allow myself—all of me—to open my senses. I am able to notice my entire body and my mind. I will become clear so I can think and articulate my actions."

Easy Guidance: Sunlight is best for this meditation. Its rays can cleanse you as well as charge your body's frequency, just as they can charge your crystals. You can also be in your safe space. I suggest it is an uncluttered space.

I like to close my eyes for this meditation. Crystals in both hands, notice if one crystal feels stronger than the other. Take a few moments to do this. Breathe in and out to get centered and open. Then sense which crystal gives you strength. Bring both hands together with the two crystals and feel the energy. If you don't feel anything, the vibrations are still working on your auric field. Breathe in and exhale slowly, really slowly. Notice the energy within your hands.

Now imagine a clean white light coming from your hands to your third eye. You can also place both crystals at that area of your forehead. The frequencies of clarity will be instilled so you can be relaxed. Now imagine white light of healing vibrations moving slowly over your physical body from the top of your head to the bottoms of your feet. Try to visualize the white light level by level, over your nose, then neck, then chest area; allow it to slowly wash over your stomach and below your belly button, then each hip, then both thighs. All the way down this white light of healing energy is moving over your shins, both your knees, and then to the ankles. Imagine feeling this vibrant energy over your feet, toes, and, now, at the bottoms of your feet. Breathe in gently and out. When you are ready, open your eyes and feel fantastic, clean, clear, and connected, body and mind.

Closing and Grounding: "I am ecstatic. I have found the perfect way to bring myself clarity. I can focus and do my best."

25. Meditation for Simplicity and Acceptance

Purpose: Erasing embedded frequencies that don't serve you from your life, such as addiction, self-pity, and self-sabotage. This meditation allows you to accept positive change without excess drama or self-sabotage or hurtful activities, thoughts, and mental disturbances.

Best Crystals: Tourmaline cleanses all negativity from one's emotional, mental, and spiritual past in this lifetime or any other. Danburite extracts embedded frequencies and gives the energy a release, which brings a void of energy that is instantaneously filled with hope and grounding so a person can move forward instead of playing the same tune of repeated frequencies.

Intention and Opening: "I am and I allow myself, on my conscious, subconscious, and soul levels, to erase any and all of my shortcomings of self-sabotage, addictive behaviors, and anything related, so that I can be me, knowing my true identity as a whole, balanced person who makes good decisions and good actions in my life. I allow this to happen today and continue every day, so my quality of life is rich and fulfilling."

Easy Guidance: This meditation is a writing meditation. You will write the intent provided below eleven times as neatly as you can and slowly repeat each word and fill in your written intention with exactly what you want to release. Try to determine which part of what you wrote you feel the most. Your indication can be a cry of release or a joy of understanding what is needed to change your life. Write exactly what you want to release. You will then add in the date, which is the day you are doing the meditation.

I am and I allow myself to let go of all negative actions and thoughts. I give myself full permission for my conscious, subconscious, and soul levels to erase any and all of my shortcomings of self-sabotage, addictive behaviors, and anything related, so that I can be me. This way I can know my true identity as a whole, balanced person who makes good decisions and good actions in life. I allow this to happen today and continue every day, so my quality of life is rich and fulfilling.

Closing and Grounding: "I am aware that I can make these positive changes in my life. I want to be shown how to adjust my attitude, my ideas of who I think I am, and I deserve to be better. I am going to be what I always was: a pure, clean, loving soul on Earth. I am easy to be friends with and likable. I am honest, trustworthy, and truthful to myself and others. I will be the best I can be. I thank myself and the universe for showing me the guidance of this change. I accept and confirm that I am who I decide to be. I am my own keeper."

Meditation without Thoughts

Autopilot is the way to meditate without thoughts. No middleman thinking involved. It is amazing to strengthen or unleash your intuitive and psychic abilities. If you are intrigued with light beings or extraterrestrial life, you can connect! Becoming mindless in a positive way to release stress or leave this dimension of time and space is possible through your mind. If you just need to step back and slow your roll, I can show you a beautiful mala or bring powerful vibrations in your energy fields with a useful tool, like a mandala! Some of us need to simply synchronize ourselves and want to know when something will occur. We can do all of this goodness with mindless meditation.

26. Meditation to Enhance Your Intuition and Psychic Abilities

Purpose: Enhance your intuition and psychic abilities to receive direct, accurate information.

Best Crystals: Labradorite—the stone that has the look of a butterfly wing—and Herkimer diamond. The mystical colors within labradorite are iridescent blues, grays, and sometimes browns. I love this intuitive third eye chakra opener. It brings enlightenment and taps your psychic abilities. Pairing labradorite with a Herkimer diamond is a *yowzer*. Herkimers are an enlightening crystal—a superstar! Herkimers amplify any other stone they are held with. Together, labradorite and Herkimer diamonds ignite your superpowers. You will be surprised when you allow your gifts to awaken while holding these crystals.

Intention and Opening: "I am and I allow myself to visit mind space, where only spirits of the light or my specific guidance comes from sources of purity. These messages are for me and to help me on my current path. My name is [full name]; please guide me with any information that can help me."

At this time, ask one question. Then notice with all your senses and body; this includes recognizing signs in your current environment and space. When you feel complete with that question, move on to the next, one at a time. I usually leave at least five minutes or longer to receive and notice before I move on to another question. I also inhale and exhale between each question and, of course, breathe normally while I am "noticing." Note that you can add your favorite archangel, ascended master, god, or goddess to receive information solely from their energy. Ask for their permission to gain information about and for you.

Easy Guidance: Choose a space that brings you the most solace, without any outside noise. This helps you notice your body's feelings and sensations. It is advantageous to notice anything you might hear or see in your mind, such as a message, a thought, or guidance. Sometimes the sensing you receive is connected to something you needed—advice or answers in the present or for your future. As you receive, write everything down and reread it later after the session is completed.

Closing and Gratitude: "I would like to thank each guide for all their expertise and sharing with me what I need to be more connected and advance my psychic abilities for the use of the greater good."

27. Meditation to Connect to Light Beings and Extraterrestrial Frequencies

Purpose: To connect to light beings and extraterrestrial frequencies.

Best Crystals: Celestite brings in soft, soothing, loving energy and sometimes calls in light beings, as does moldavite. These frequencies allow telepathic communication with those from other atmospheres.

Intention and Opening: "I am and I allow myself to connect to [light or extraterrestrial beings]. I will be able to sense them and understand messages from my intuitive abilities and my sensitivities of hearing, feeling, and inner knowing. When I fully wake, I will take notes on my sensations and thoughts, which are messages from them to me."

Easy Guidance: Breathe in and out to relax your body. Do this at a nice, slow pace. At least six breaths in and out. As you find yourself completely relaxed, notice your third eye and visualize white light opening that area of your forehead. It is easy and light and feels beautiful. This will allow a connection for you and your communicators to telepathically send you information that you can clearly understand.

As you relax and feel the white light over the top of your head and forehead, you feel safe and warm. Your body from the nose all the way down to your feet is feeling activated with a heavenly pink light of energy. This makes you feel comfortable. Your shoulders feel like you are receiving a hug from your guides and friends of the light. They will start to show you visions or help you get a color or picture as a message. You may also hear something or feel as though they are speaking to you in your inner mind. Occasionally you may feel a soft touch on the forehead or shoulder. This is them letting you know they are present.

Allow and receive. If you are completely relaxed and would like to, imagine a rope or energy rope that looks like light. You can grab this rope and allow your visitors to pull you into a space where they reside. You can do this by asking them to bring you into this space safely.

When you are ready to come back to Earth, mindfully ask them to bring you back safely.

Closing and Gratitude: "I would like to thank all the beings who brought me wonderful visions and experiences. I am back and hope to continue a space travel with you soon."

28. Mindlessness Meditation

Purpose: To let go of any restrictive thoughts or feelings that bind you emotionally or mentally.

Best Crystals: Apophyllite and moldavite take you to a mind space of bliss out of the body. Apophyllite, the unicorn crystal, opens the third eye to experiences that are out of this world. Moldavite can lift your spirit from your physical body to float into space for amazing journeys of the mind and beyond.

Intention and Opening: "I am and I allow myself to become mindless for this meditation that brings me to my beautiful energy of freedom and light."

Easy Guidance: For this meditation, lie faceup and place the apophyllite on your third eye. If it falls or moves during the meditation, just let it; don't worry about replacing it. Just be where you are. Place the moldavite anywhere from your chest area up to your head.

Once you are lying down, place a blanket near or over you. This makes most people feel safe and relaxed. When you are comfortable, imagine a light blue light and a violet light. Both are side by side, flowing from your feet to your head, keeping you warm and safe. This blue light is powerful. Understand that the vibrations of this particular blue light will make you weightless. The violet light is just as strong. You may begin to float or fall asleep. Just allow it. You will reach your nothingness and most likely feel incredible as you wake.

Closing and Gratitude: "I am back in my physical earthly body and I enjoy floating to my mindless space. I know I can visit this space anytime I wish, but for now I am back and grounded, appreciating life."

29. Releasing Stress Meditation

Purpose: Releasing negative thought patterns that can bind you and keep you stuck in worry and anguish. This meditation will help you become Zen and balanced. If you are having one of those days when it seems everything you do or say brings an upset, this meditation can create a neutralizing frequency, then bring you back to balance.

Best Crystals: Apophyllite opens the third eye and all the chakras to accept clarity, enlightenment, and newness. Tourmaline protects, cleanses, and rids you of all negativity on all layers of your aura as it squeaky-cleans your chakras!

Intention and Opening: "I am and I allow myself to release all thoughts that are not positive. I can use today to think and say only positive words and scenarios about myself. I stay in the present with my thoughts and my amazing future. I allow myself to go outside my present and into an incredible journey in my mind, to release, let go, and just have some amusement."

Easy Guidance: The best way to release stress is to go somewhere else in your mind. The tourmaline will release the negatives and the apophyllite will take you someplace magnificent. This is a journey that takes you away from negativity and brings out your imagination. You can sit or lie down for this meditation.

It's time to daydream. Allow yourself to visualize this place, knowing you are safe and loved. You are here on your mini vacation. Accept it. Imagine walking on soft grass where there was once a path. You are feeling adventurous and decide to walk forward on that path. Step by step, you are breathing in the air. It's sunny and just the right temperature for you.

The sky is bright blue and butterflies are abundant. You can see that there is a cluster of flowers off to your right by a big oak tree. The flowers are red, pink, and yellow. Everything is very bright and bountiful. You continue walking on that path forward. You can now see a pond on your right. You see a wooden bench near a shady tree budding with wispy, light pink flowers. You decide to go off the path and gaze at all those beautiful sights: the flowers, the tree, the pond, and the butterflies.

You sit comfortably on the wooden bench where the flowers from the tree are shading you but not touching you. As you look down on the bench, you see writing carved into it. You read the message. At that exact moment, you realize that message is from you. It somehow is letting you know that everything in your life is fine. That your life really is positive. It was no coincidence that you were meant to sit on that bench at that pond. You feel loved, watched over, and protected. You sit and enjoy those emotions for as long as you wish.

Later when you are ready to move on, you return to the grassy path. You walk about five hundred feet before you notice an animal. It is gentle and just wanted you to know it was there. The animal looks at you, and you are locking eyes. You both feel safe and peaceful about the connection. You feel as if this animal is trying to speak to you. You close your eyes and ask, "What are you trying to tell me?"

When you open your eyes, the animal is gone, but you feel like you heard what the animal was saying to you. It was a message you longed to hear: "You are appreciated." It was a heartfelt moment. You look around for the animal one more time, but it is gone. You decide it's time to go back the way you came. Again, walking that fresh grass path past the pond, the pink wispy tree, and the bench. You pass the butterflies and flowers back to your original starting point. You take a huge breath in, and a huge breath out, feeling loved, appreciated, and revitalized. It's time to open your eyes and be pleased that you are who you are. You will only think positive thoughts, because you know that if you want to, you can.

Closing and Gratitude: "I am grateful to have a mini journey, a vacation in my mind that takes me to a happy place where I can feel loved by the universe."

30. Meditations to Leave Time and Space

Purpose: To pursue another location or dimension that brings you serenity or self-realization of a lifetime that could be affecting this current lifetime. You can choose the intent that matches your need.

Best Crystals: Moldavite helps lift you out of the body into a bliss state or uninhibited frequency. Apophyllite also uplifts you while adding the enhancement of visual, vivid, clear frequencies, making your outer space trip unique.

Intention and Opening One: "I am and allow myself to visit a dimension that brings me peace and serenity beyond my life on Earth. I will come back safely as I am protected on my travels."

Intention and Opening Two: "I am and I allow myself to revisit a life that is pertinent to my current life's actions and feelings. I will have a strong self-realization with a positive outlook from what I experience. I am safe and protected as I explore and will remember what I need to for insight on this current lifetime."

Easy Guidance: In your comfort zone, trust that all is good and protected with your choice of intention and opening. I suggest playing music without words. Ambiance music or nature sound is best. Imagine you are floating, light as a feather, moving through the soft wind and up, up, up! You can float. This is amazing, as your body may feel stable while your mind is open and willing to reach another space or time.

This lightness of the mind will keep going higher and higher to the sky and then become one with the stars and planets. You can stay in that peaceful, safe bliss or continue to move to the Milky Way. This space takes you into another dimension that brings you to a life that you have been connected to previously.

Imagine opening a door from that upper level of space in the sky. As you walk through the door, you will experience a lifetime that you have lived. Enjoy the life; notice who you are or what you might be doing or associated with. Do you live alone or with family? Are you working or at home? Try to feel your age and what you may be doing and speaking to. This will give you wonderful insight, and as you continue, there will be a moment when you feel it is time to come back to where you started. Float back to the level of the stars and planets, then down, back into the realm of Earth, back to your starting point at your Zen space.

Closing and Gratitude: "I am appreciative of my ability to travel outside to other dimensions in my mind. It helps me with my current life and enables me to feel more fulfilled with my earthly duties and life."

31. Meditation with a Mala to Slow Your Roll

Purpose: To slow your mind and recapture peaceful moments in your life. If you are usually too far ahead of yourself and you need to give yourself time to breathe. If you are making lots of mistakes or not listening to or hearing other people around you because you are multitasking or too busy for anything in your life. Do you feel guilty when you are doing something for yourself? This meditation is for you. This is also good to do if you don't know what to do with yourself when you're not working.

Best Crystals: Amethyst is relaxing and soothing, allowing you to keep the vibe of serenity. Rose quartz brings in the frequency of love, compassion, and energy for this meditation. Mala beads are preferably strung with 108 beads.

Intention and Opening: "I am and I allow myself to slow my mind but also to be intelligent, alert, and methodical as needed. I can relax my thoughts by writing down any task I have. I can do them one by one, in the timing that suits me, to correctly do my best with ease."

Easy Guidance: At this time, if you are thinking you should be doing five other things instead of this meditation, write out what you need to do so you will not forget them. Then you can allow yourself to relax the mind and body. Once you have completed the list, set it away from you, at least ten feet in distance. Then get yourself comfy, sitting on a mat, pillow, or recliner. Set your intent and opening once again. Give yourself some words of gratitude for allowing yourself this time. "I do deserve this relaxing time for myself."

If you have an amethyst mala, hold it in your hands. Then, close your eyes and touch the first bead. You are going to be touching each bead separately. Start counting each one. As you say "number one," take a big breath in and breathe out as slowly as you can before you go to "number two." Continue with the breaths in and out until you get to the last bead. You want to take your time; it's about relaxing with each breath in and out. By the time you reach the 108th bead, you will be revitalized.

If you would like to stop there, that is fine. You have done a great self-meditation. If you would like to continue, keep your hands on that last bead and start counting backward and touching each bead. Continue with the breaths in and out until you reach the "number one" bead.

Closing and Gratitude: "I am thankful for this time I give myself to relax and slow down. I feel revitalized and relaxed at the same time, which proves I can give myself peace in slowing my everyday roll."

32. Meditation with a Mandala

Purpose: Mandalas attract positive vibrations in a unified shape or form of art. This can uplift your frequency. The gift of the mandala is that it holds unique frequencies and gives off its energy to the holder and gazer! You can hold a natural flower, like a rose. A rose is a form of sacred geometry because of its DNA makeup. You can feel the energy from its natural formation. You can also use a painted or printed mandala or a crystal on top of a flower of life mandala, which is doubly optimal in raising your frequencies super fast.

Best Crystals: Any geometric crystal or a quartz crystal brings in high vibrations to create positive frequencies within your electromagnetic fields, uplifting your energy to be more balanced and focused. You can use a copy of a flower of life mandala for this meditation. You can also go to Crystaljunkie.com and download a free channeled mandala for your meditation. If you would like to use an earth element, a flower of any type is considered a mandala, which is sacred geometry.

Intention and Opening: "I am and I allow myself to bring in positive vibrations to my mind, body, and soul. I can connect with this geometric shape to gather insights, self-clarity, and my own personal powerful mindset."

Easy Guidance: Once you are set and sitting comfortably, place your mandala in front of you where it is easy to view. Place your geometric crystal in one of your hands or beside the mandala.

Take three long, deep breaths and three long exhales. If you have essences on your hands, breathe them in. Exhale on each breath very slowly.

Now gaze at the mandala. Hold your hands three inches over the middle of the mandala. Feel the energy from the mandala move to your hands. Notice if you are feeling and receiving.

Now close your eyes. Let whatever comes into your mind come. It may be colors, a message, a picture—like a movie of something. Just be. Breathe in and out, and keep yourself relaxed.

When you are ready, look once more at the mandala, hands over it again. Stay as long as you like. Take a deep breath in and exhale any energy that you feel inclined to. Then, close your meditation.

Closing and Gratitude: "I am grateful for all of your loving presence. I would like to thank all the guides from the light and healer guides here today. Thank you. I am grateful for the high vibrational energies to heal and advance myself. I would like to give my thanks to all of you and the crystal energies for the powerful healing of the mandala. This sacred geometry was used only with loving intentions. I am well. Gratitude."

33. Meditation to Synchronize the Self and Ask When Something Will Occur

Purpose: Meditation can bring you to that "knowing." This type of meditation is when you "talk" to all parts of you and find out when something will occur. The soul energy of you, your conscious, and subconscious all collaborate and come to the same page. This is how your "self" can be better at making decisions. Or at least come up with positive temporary or permanent solutions (along with receiving partial or complete solutions). This mindful meditation will help you sync to when something can occur. Think of it as a telepathic conference call—to have clear understanding where all of us connect to make compromises or move ahead with anything that is for the greater good. Keep in mind that your soul knows and wants what is best for you; it's the other two you need to keep in line (conscious and subconscious)! Sometimes those ones go wild!

This is an intuitive meditation, assisting you in asking a single question for you, to you. It sounds like a tongue twister, but it really is enlightening if it's something you would like to know.

Here is a side story to get a point across. I have a client who has been trying to "decide" for years if she should leave her husband. She is never grounded, never able to see clearly and situate her true feelings about the situation. Her vibration is lower than normal because she holds these frequencies of fear. She started to realize it was her mind that she needed to shift. After a few minutes of grounding herself, she would voice to me that she knows what she should do and wants to do about the situation. This was repeated over several years. Each time she would be ready after her grounding, but I would see her a month or so later, and she would be back to square one.

Grounding is amazing. It gives us clarity and strength, a feeling of security, and a solution. But (this is a big but), if you don't stay grounded, you'll have a downfall. It is also the practice of "talking" to all aspects of self (your soul, conscious, and subconscious) on a regular basis that keeps you in the truth of your life. Basically, you can get the epiphanies in these high-vibe moments, then release them by your own accord. Staying on the high vibe brings power and confidence along with happiness, teaching you that you can do what you want and need. That "knowing" of what is best for your happiness is a high vibration that can be permanent if you choose to adopt it as your frequency.

So you can see how people repeat, repeat, repeat. Sometimes the universe steps in and takes it out of their hands. This we call "divine intervention." But why not take hold of your own happiness? Some people repeat until the situation is decided by others involved, such as the spouse in that situation. Many times, the sadness or incompleteness brings a person to a depressed or unhealthy state, to a low vibration of unhappiness. There is a way out: high vibrations that are constant.

Best Crystals: Labradorite is a crystal that enhances and opens your psychic abilities. Unakite brings forth all aspects of you and knowledge of self to be revealed. This is where it gets good, because all you have to do is ask yourself nicely while being in a high vibrational state of mind.

Intention and Opening: "I am and I allow myself to get off my roller coaster that goes round and round. I want to stop repeating my same story to myself and others about my unhappiness. I want to be happy and move on in my life. I also want to ask about the timing of when I will be ready to shift to my new life."

Easy Guidance: Start by tapping your feet on the ground and stating, "I am present on Earth and I am glad to be here today." This is a small grounding self-talk. The action of tapping your feet makes your subconscious realize that it is part of this call. Now you are ready to call in all of you: "I call in my soul energy, my conscious, and my subconscious. My name is [full name]. I want to make sure all of me is present." You should feel a *yes*. This could be a vision, a tingle, or heat in any part of your body.

Continue by saying, "We are all here and connecting with a circle as our line of conversing." You now will imagine a circle of green light for loving energy. You can also draw a green circle on a piece of paper and write in it that each part of you is present for this meeting. Then say, "I am now addressing all of us with a question. [Ask a specific question.] I would like to specifically and accurately know when this shift will occur."

Visualize the questions as if they were a segment in a movie. This way they become real, and you are mindful in what you are asking. As you inquire, notice the first feeling or vision or anything that pops into your head. Write it down or note it in your mind. This is not a long meditation; it is quick and to the point. You can always ask about more than one question, but some people start overthinking it, and then the answers start coming from the subconscious, and sometimes it doesn't play fair. Sometimes it fibs. All need to be present and freshly ready to answer accurately.

Closing and Gratitude: "I am proud that all of me—soul, conscious, and subconscious—have connected and brought forth information for my greater good and all involved. I trust the timing and am ready to shift. Thank you."

I hope you enjoyed the meditations and that you come back frequently to be in your bliss. It is surprising and fun to know that these little moments of time you invest in yourself will make a huge difference in your life. Just remember you can always continue the meditative practices on a deeper level.

Chapter 9
Continuing the Meditation Process

Did you absolutely love the techniques and choices of meditations that were offered? I'll bet you did. You had to have felt that *bliss* I was talking about. That peace of mind and urge to stay in that *space* just a bit longer.

After you have completed your meditation practice, I suggest journaling or jotting down some insights you may have had. How did you feel? Happy? Excited? Motivated? Do you have a sense of release? You may just feel grateful or relaxed. Whatever you feel, note it, because reading your notes later on will help you realize things about yourself. This begins the connection of knowing your body on all levels.

Speaking of levels, did you remember to write down your frequency number before and after your meditation? If you forgot, please do it the next time you meditate. Your progress will surely amaze you. No one is judging you as you raise your vibes and adjust your frequencies daily or weekly! When I started meditating, my frequency was a true five. Within a week of meditating, I stayed a steady eight. Today, I am a ten—see how self-kudos works! Truthfully, I look forward to the time I give myself daily. I can say meditation is my self-passion. Meditation brings me to my level of contentment.

Note what type of meditation you practiced in case you want to do the same one again. Each time you meditate can be quite different, and keeping a progression log is advantageous. Especially if you noticed any shifts with your perceptions, your thoughts, and your overall energy. It can be a physical change or an emotional shift.

The mental part is interesting. I noticed that I shifted emotionally as I became stronger with my focus and decision-making the more I meditated. The method I used was a bit of all of them. I like to change it up so I don't get bored. Sometimes I make my own concoction of meditations, adding a mindful meditation in the morning and a mindless type at night. I would do an active meditation, like the walking meditation, once a week, then mid-week I would connect with my higher self, and sometimes on the same mid-week day I would manifest.

By the time I get to the weekend, I like to take off to a faraway place on a dimensional travel just before I go to sleep. This way, my mind is strong and my body and soul are connecting as a weekly practice—a healthy habit.

I wrote a reminder in my phone or on my fridge to keep on track with my meditation. It actually is part of my self-passion percentage because I love meditation and I feel it's a treat for myself to be able to spend time with my guides, self, and other beings.

If you are a super detailed and goal-oriented person, this is a perfect way to keep it organized. Keep a chart to describe how your senses have been accentuated or accelerated. You can notice if you have become sharper in your work tasks or if your body feels less tension and emotional stress. You can also list daily how you let go of occurrences that might have had your undies in a bunch had you not meditated that day!

It's just good practice and fun to jot and journal your success. I have one client who journals her happiness from her weekly meditation practice. She writes a happy face every time she meditates instead of stress eating! She lost the weight she wanted to and has been keeping it off without emotionally fighting herself since she started using the five methods of meditating.

Sample Journaling

Here is a sample of jotting my meditation down.

Date: [Date]

Meditation: Walking, gratitude, and manifesting.

My frequency before the meditation: 8

My frequency after the meditation: 10—whoop whoop!

Notes: I felt so high on life and nature. I felt confident and secure as I walked to my favorite tree and back. When I touched the tree, it made me feel happy and powerful. I feel an inner knowing that what I asked for will come true on the date I requested. I also felt my friends who have passed into the light visit me as I was giving gratitude to them. Feeling very loved and protected today.

Emoji: Super happy face ☺.

If I had done a different method of meditation, such as a channeling meditation for higher knowledge, it would be as follows:

Date: [Date]

My frequency before the meditation: 7

My frequency after the meditation: 10

Scribbles of my insight or messages: [Messages I received.]

Notes: Archangel Michael says I will complete my goals in the month of June this year. I felt in my heart chakra that it will be, and I had chills on my arms. I felt another visitor who was angelic as well. This felt like a female energy who wanted to let me know I am strong.

Journaling is something you can look back on whenever. It shows you who you are and how you live. It brings you up and lets you know when you need to shift. It helps your gift of life stay healthy and balanced. When you emit high vibes, you attract what you desire and better yourself; on top of that, you spread your happy vibes to those around you, inspiring others. We all affect one another—spread the meditations and share frequencies that rock!

Expansion

When we look back on our jottings or journals, it helps us see how we have shifted and lets us see and feel more complete in life. Think of it as expansion.

Expansion of the mind is allowing yourself to continue the process of learning and igniting your enlightenment that there is more than what we see. There is a whole world within worlds in our minds. Expanding the vision beyond your eyes is a practice. Know that your imagination is the truth of the all-knowing you. I wouldn't know what to do with myself if I couldn't expand my knowledge of what is and what could be manifesting.

This takes me to loving my mindset. I can program myself to have positive or negative thoughts, attitudes, or actions. It's all me. It's all my frequency. Every thought is energy—a frequency that can be accepted or changed. I choose to keep my vibes loving and kind. Once an experience or occurrence gets me offtrack, I remember I am in charge of how I feel and react. I am in control of me. I decide to choose loving frequencies.

Life isn't about what you can make other people do for you, it is about what you do for yourself with all that exists. If this resonates with you, then you have a good understanding that you can meditate easily. Because meditation is just that—having equal energy to feel and experience without conflict or interruptions. It is peace. I assume that is why many philosophers say meditation gives us peace of mind. It actually is using a piece of our mind that we never exercise. Let's change that. I completed easy techniques to get you to that free space.

The next step is practice, practice, practice. Practice using every method and each purposeful meditation. As you take this journey, you will master "you." When you can meditate with a train going by, a neighbor's grass trimmer buzzing, outside noise, or your inner thoughts' noise, that is bliss. I will personally crown you a master of meditation. Nothing can separate you from your serenity connection. Once you've gotten that uncovered, you are limitless.

Recommended Resources

Crystals

DeMarco, Jolie. *My Daily Crystal*. Self-published, 2017. https://apps.apple.com/us/app/my-daily-crystal/id1292417752.

Simons, Robert, and Naisha Ahsian. *Stones of the New Consciousness*. East Montpelier, VT: Heaven and Earth Publishing, 2015.

Meditations

DeMarco, Jolie. *Archangel Michael's 7 Heavenly Guided Meditations*. Self-published, 2017. https://crystaljunkie.com/guidedmeditations/.

Pond, David. *Chakras for Beginners*. Woodbury, MN: Llewellyn Publications, 1999.

Wix, Angela. *Llewellyn's Little Book of Unicorns*. Woodbury, MN: Llewellyn Publications, 2019.

Bibliography

Corliss, Julie. "Mindfulness Meditation May Ease Anxiety, Mental Stress." *Harvard Health Publishing*. January 8, 2014. https://www.health.harvard.edu/blog/mindfulness-meditation-may-ease-anxiety-mental-stress-201401086967.

Cousto, Hans. "The Planetary and Chakra Frequencies." http://www.luminanti.com/SYNOPSIS%20Planetary%20and%20Chakra%20%20Frequencies.pdf.

DeMarco, Jolie. *High-Vibe Crystal Healing*. Woodbury, MN: Llewellyn Publications, 2019.

———. *Soul Talking and Relationships*. Boca Raton, FL: Self-published, 2010.

"Energy." *Britannica*. https://www.britannica.com/science/energy.

Gienger, Michael. *Healing Crystals: The A–Z Guide to 430 Gemstones*. Scotland: Findhorn Press, 2005.

———. *Healing Crystals: Power of Healing*. London: Octopus Publishing Group, 1998.

Jung, Carl. *The Archetypes and The Collective Unconscious*. 2nd ed. Princeton, NJ: Princeton University, 1980.

"Mandala." *Merriam-Webster*. https://www.merriam-webster.com/dictionary/mandala.

"Merkaba Symbol." *Ancient-Symbols.com*. https://www.ancient-symbols.com/symbols-directory/merkaba.html.

Vogt, Kate. *Mala of the Heart: 108 Sacred Poems*. New World Library, 2015.

To Write to the Author

If you wish to contact the author or would like more information about this book, please write to the author in care of Llewellyn Worldwide Ltd. and we will forward your request. Both the author and the publisher appreciate hearing from you and learning of your enjoyment of this book and how it has helped you. Llewellyn Worldwide Ltd. cannot guarantee that every letter written to the author can be answered, but all will be forwarded. Please write to:

Jolie DeMarco
℅ Llewellyn Worldwide
2143 Wooddale Drive
Woodbury, MN 55125-2989

Please enclose a self-addressed stamped envelope for reply,
or $1.00 to cover costs. If outside the U.S.A., enclose
an international postal reply coupon.

Many of Llewellyn's authors have websites with additional
information and resources. For more information,
please visit our website at http://www.llewellyn.com.

Notes

Notes

Notes

Notes

Notes